COOK WILD

Susanne Fischer-Rizzi

COOK WILD

Year-round cooking on an open fire

Photographs by Sabine Mader
and Ulrike Schmid

F

FRANCES LINCOLN LIMITED
PUBLISHERS

Frances Lincoln Limited
4 Torriano Mews
Torriano Avenue
London NW5 2RZ
www.franceslincoln.com

Cook Wild
Text copyright © Susanne Fischer-Rizzi
Photographs copyright © Sabine Mader and Ulrike Schmid

First published in Germany in 2010 as *Wilde Küche* by AT Verlag
First Frances Lincoln edition 2012

A catalogue record for this book is available from the British Library

ISBN 978-0-7112-3281-5

Printed and bound in China

9 8 7 6 5 4 3 2 1

Disclaimer

Gather only wild food that you can identify with certainty; when in
doubt, consult a local expert. Take into account local regulations
for gathering food and for the use of fire. Neither the author nor the
publisher can accept any legal responsibility for any harm, injury,
loss, damage or prosecution resulting from the use or misuse of the
techniques, tools and advice in this book.

CONTENTS

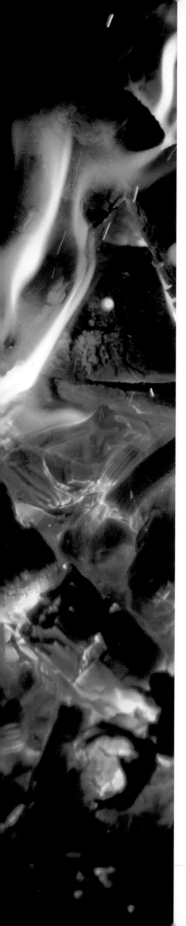

INTRODUCTION
A Touch of Adventure

Cooking on an open fire is an activity that gives me enormous pleasure. It means spending time outdoors with family and friends, or enjoying a solitary meal by the fire; it means cooking sometimes in a simple and archaic way as our forefathers did, and sometimes like modern gourmet chefs, but always with minimal effort. I may cook dishes from around the world or traditional dishes prepared according to old, almost-forgotten recipes. Nature is my kitchen – a kitchen so practical, original and sensual that any modern high-tech kitchen is dwarfed in comparison and the microwave becomes a soulless appliance. The outdoor kitchen offers a multifaceted experience for the senses: the spicy scents of the fire and the wood waft into my nose; the gentle crackling of the flames gives me a feeling of security; the heat pleasantly warms my cheeks. The vast firmament spreads out over everything like an immense blanket. As I cook and eat I can enjoy the landscape or just stretch out and relax in the grass – and of course the unexpected can never be ruled out. The outdoor kitchen never ceases to fascinate, for one cannot escape the mysterious magic of fire – which is the heart of wild cuisine.

There is room for everyone in the kitchen under the open sky. It invites people to sit together, chat, listen and participate. The open fire has been instrumental in fostering relationships and hospitality, and protecting the community, from earliest times. Today, cooking on an open fire is still an occasion for a social get-together at which all generations feel at ease. Especially now, when traditional social structures are disappearing, when family meals are sometimes even eaten in front of the television, cooking on an open fire and eating together can greatly enhance both leisure time and relationships.

The campfire brings back the best of our childhood memories, and being close to the fire brings out the child within us. Children are fascinated by fire and are always eager to participate. A campfire conveys to them the joy of outdoor life, which is often lacking in their lives, usually through want of opportunity. Children need to experience an elementary, immediate and genuine closeness to fire, as well as to nature as a whole; otherwise they lose their awareness of the natural world.

Open fires are no longer part of our daily lives, and are now so laden with taboos and restrictions that they have almost completely disappeared. In my opinion, however, the campfire is one of the things we should protect from extinction.

The place where you cook and eat, even temporarily, becomes your home. So by cooking on an open fire nature and the wild cease to be surroundings. This leads to a richer experience of nature, and a deep, pleasing and comforting association. The further we move away from nature in our everyday lives, the greater is the healing power of time spent outdoors without pressure to achieve. By cooking under the open sky we can discover a new living space and spend time relaxing in it.

I would like to invite you to join me at fires under the open sky, for only time spent outdoors reveals nature to us in all its beauty and enables us to rid ourselves of the pressures of everyday life. When cooking on an open fire, we can take time out from civilization. In our high-tech world and complex lives, it is simple things that bring real relaxation and pleasure. In the 'wild kitchen' we do without high-tech things, and this creates the opportunity for improvisation and experiment. It allows us to enjoy simple things, and seasons them with romance, nostalgia and the spirit of adventure.

In the outdoor kitchen you are occasionally visited by animals, since you are in their world. It is amazing and exhilarating to watch how animals react when they see us humans pause and take time for contemplation, and to feel in tune with a place. If we do this we can watch birds, admire butterflies, see a fox scurrying past or discover a deer peeking out from behind a bush.

Many people associate an outdoor fire with summer. The outdoor kitchen, however, is open in all seasons. For that reason the recipes in this book are grouped by seasons. Each season has its own flavour, culinary quality and attractions. You can enjoy a cheese fondue with snowflakes in winter, a stew in the mist in autumn or a night-time picnic by full moon in summer, or wake up to the scent of campfire coffee in spring.

Cooking on an open fire is one of the oldest of the human arts. The earliest fireplaces discovered in Africa date back around 1.5 million years. On prehistoric fireplaces humans once prepared the meat of hippos, giraffes, wild boar and gazelles. Taking into account the differences between the jaw of prehistoric man and the human jaw today, we can assume that food was cooked on an open fire from as long as 2 million years ago. So man has grilled, cooked and baked his meals on an open fire for a very long time. But the fire used by early man is the same as the fire used in the outdoor kitchen today, and it still fulfils the same function. This may be the reason for our continuing desire to light a fire and cook on it; perhaps prehistoric fireplaces are the origin – like an ancient heritage – of our joy in playing with fire.

In the long period of time since the first fireplaces until today, various cooking techniques for the open fire have been developed, and a rich repertoire of recipes has been passed down to us. Only the things that really worked have survived all this time. In this book you will find many of these cooking methods, which you can try out with lots of different recipes. Follow the trails of our Stone Age ancestors, sit at a fire and enjoy some Stone Age soup together; or prepare a dish in a Dutch oven and let it take you back in time on a culinary trek westwards with the American pioneers. I have chosen my favourites from the abundant recipes for cooking on an open fire. I hope the book will inspire and encourage you to let your imagination run free.

When you cook under the open sky, there is usually a herb garden right next to you. So you can take up

nature's friendly offer and enhance your dishes with wild herbs. You will find a chapter on this (page 26), as well as suitable recipes and appropriate tips for each season.

Much of our food nowadays is pre-prepared: it contains additives, artificial flavouring and often preservatives. The recipes in my 'wild cuisine' do not require these. Whenever possible, I use organic products, out of a sense of responsibility and respect for nature: organically grown local vegetables, organic meat, native vegetable oil, premium natural salt and whole peppercorns crushed between two stones just before use. This is not only good for you, but gives the food a more natural flavour, as you would expect from outdoor cooking.

Outdoor cooking also means travelling light, as our ancestors did when they were still leading a nomadic life. Unlike them, though, we do not have to cover long distances through rough country to hunt for a mammoth steak. We can enjoy hiking, biking, walking with snowshoes or travelling by car, mobile home, boat or canoe, with a tent. In the course of any of these outdoor activities, you may find yourself in an inhospitable place and have to feed yourself, with very few resources available, and this book will show you how you can prepare a delicious meal on an open fire with very little effort. Or you may simply want to enjoy good food outdoors.

The very act of lighting a fire out in the wild and marvelling at its flames will make you feel part of the great natural world. Embrace the adventure it offers and live the experience to the full!

FIRE: THE HEART OF THE OUTDOOR KITCHEN

Taming the fire devil

Fire has both nourishing and destructive qualities, so to avoid accidents you must treat this hot, unpredictable element responsibly and with caution. To cook on an open fire you must be able to control a fire with confidence. Here are some useful basic tips.

The fireplace

Consider your choice of a place for a fire carefully, always thinking of your safety as well as protecting the countryside. A fire in an inappropriate place can be dangerous. Use existing, authorized fireplaces or barbecue areas wherever they are available.

When building a new fire, avoid the following:

- places with overhanging, especially dry branches
- the vicinity of dead trees with dry wood
- dry grass or a dried-out meadow
- places with overhanging rocks (heat can cause rocks to loosen and fall).

Never light a fire on dry peaty soil, moss or tree roots, where the fire could continue to burn underground for days or even weeks and subsequently cause a smouldering fire. The best types of ground for a fire are sand, gravel or earth. If the ground is damp, light the fire on top of branches and twigs.

Leave as few traces as possible: this is the motto for considerate fire making. You could, for instance, cut out a section of turf to make your fireplace; if you do, set it aside so that you can replace it after you have finished – it will grow back in relatively quickly. The best way to avoid leaving traces of a fire on the ground is to use a firebowl. This is usually made of metal and should have legs long enough for it to be positioned stably on the ground. A firebowl makes it possible to light a fire in many places where this would otherwise be prohibited. Firebowls are available in many shapes and sizes in camping supply shops. A hobo oven (see page 21) is another good alternative where making fires is not allowed.

Consider also that the fire is the heart of the outdoor kitchen, where you spend quite some time preparing food, but also relaxing. You should therefore choose a place where you feel comfortable.

Fire and wind

Pay attention to the wind direction. Sparks can fly and reach distant dry material such as dead trees or even a barn. Choose a sheltered place for your fire. Protect the fire against wind by making a circle of stones around it. Do not use damp or wet stones for this, as they may explode. You can also use the stones as a rest for grills, jugs, pots and pans. When it is very windy, light your fire in the centre of a pit.

Flames, embers and ashes

The kind of fire you need will depend on the cooking method you intend to use. The cooking fire has three cooking zones: flames, embers and ashes. You will be primarily using one of those, and which one you want to use will determine how you make your fire.

For cooking with pots and pans you will need only a small fire with flames no more than a finger length long. The temperature will be hottest directly above the flames.

If you need mainly embers that will last, it is best to make a keyhole fireplace. Expand the circle of stones around the fire into the shape of a keyhole, creating two large surface areas connected by a narrow passage. You burn wood constantly in the larger space, and transfer the resulting embers to the narrower space, where you can then bake or cook. The more embers you need, the larger your fireplace should be.

Leave as few traces as possible
Do not leave the fire until the fire and embers have been completely extinguished. So always make sure you start letting the fire burn down early enough, and then extinguish it with sand and water.

As well as replacing any turf you have removed when you have finished, take any litter home with you – even that of others – rather than leaving it behind. Remove all traces of the fire.

Rules and regulations
Every country and region has its own regulations regarding outdoor fires. Make sure you have all the appropriate information before you light a fire. Also take into account that there are certain times when fires are prohibited because of the increased risk of forest fires.

WOOD: HEAT, FLAVOUR AND AMBIENCE

Kitchen or living room?

The heart of the wild kitchen does not beat without wood. When gathering wood, you need make an informed and well-considered selection. Do you want your fire to serve as a light source, for heat or for cooking? Do you want to bake, smoke or grill? Depending on your requirements, choose the type of wood with appropriate burning properties.

It is also useful to know which type of wood produces quick heat and which long-lasting heat. If you are very hungry, you do not want to wait for hours until the fire has produced the desired amount of embers. For a quick fire, use finger-thick twigs and large logs. Some types of wood produce less light and take longer to produce a lot of embers. This means that you will have to wait longer before eating, but you will have plenty of time to prepare the food. The cooking method also influences your choice of wood: for a clay oven (see page 23) you will need a different type of wood from that for cooking on a board or a leaf.

Fire is also a heat source; we want to be close to it, especially in winter – perhaps when we are enjoying some mulled wine. Therefore it is also good to know which type of wood to choose for a fire that will produce more heat.

Finally, the type of wood, its smoke and aromas, can influence the flavour of the food we grill or smoke in our outdoor kitchen.

The open fire is our kitchen, but also our living room; it is where we prepare our meals, make ourselves comfortable, tell stories and relax.

Lighting and atmosphere are important factors, and each type of wood creates distinct lighting and atmosphere. The atmosphere at an open fire is as variable as the wood you burn: reflective, powerful, moving, calming, melancholy or comforting. Some types of wood produce a bright light and are excellent for cooking and conviviality, while others produce a more muted light, creating a dreamier atmosphere. All these types are explained below.

We all know the following situation: you are sitting by the fire in calm weather and the smoke is in your face. You change sides, and the smoke is still in your face. This irritating phenomenon is created by the low air pressure that develops between you and the fire, sucking in the hot air together with the smoke. You can avoid this by creating another low-pressure zone on the other side of the fire. Simply put up a tarpaulin or lay a canoe on its side with the open side facing the fire – it should be slightly larger than the people sitting on the other side of the fire.

Gathering wood

Before starting a fire, gather enough wood and lay out everything you need. If there is no wood near by, or gathering it is forbidden, bring your own. It should be well seasoned and dry. Do not forget to bring an axe, to make chippings for starting the fire.

Lighting a fire

You do not need artificial firelighters to start a fire. Because of its high terpene content, the paper-thin outer bark of beech burns like paper, even in damp weather. Other natural dry material which makes good tinder includes grass panicles, dandelion,

poplar and willow seeds, dry foliage, lichen, dry nettle fibre, dry fern leaves and tree resin. Lay logs parallel to each other, put a bundle of brushwood over them, place the tinder on them and pile dry twigs loosely in the form of a pyramid on top. This will get a good draught going for the fire, as in a chimney. Now light the tinder and gradually add larger logs.

You will find dry wood particularly near conifers. You can break brushwood and dead twigs directly off tree trunks. Good dry wood makes a hollow cracking sound when you break it. Do not break living branches off trees.

The different qualities of wood

Softwood burns quickly and is ideal for lighting a fire and fast cooking. Hardwood, on the other hand, burns slowly but provides a more lasting heat and

very hot embers. Conifer wood burns quickly because of its high resin content, but produces a lot of smoke and sparks. You should therefore not use conifer wood such as larch, pine or fir for a fire if you wish to sleep next to it, as glowing pieces of wood could fly out of the fire and burn holes in your camping mats and sleeping bags. Do not wear clothes made of synthetic fibres for cooking at an open fire, as they are highly flammable. Deciduous wood produces fewer sparks. It is good for smoking, as it gives the food an additional flavour. You should never burn plywood or pressure-impregnated woods, as they produce poisonous fumes.

Hardwood: larch, oak, beech, ash, maple, elm
Softwood: poplar, lime, willow, birch, spruce, pine
Conifer wood: spruce, fir, larch, pine, juniper
Deciduous wood: beech, birch, willow, maple, alder, ash, fruit trees

Types of firewood suitable for outdoor cooking

Alder: easy to light, burns down quickly, good for smoking.

Apple: good for smoking and grilling, adds flavour. Gather after pruning.

Ash: burns easily and slowly; good ember formation, nice flames, hardly any sparks.

Beech: less easily flammable, burns slowly with few sparks; gives a lot of heat and long-lasting embers; beautiful bright flames; excellent wood for smoking.

Birch: also burns when wet and fresh. Burns bright and hot with beautiful light-blue flames; warms well, gives few embers; hardly sparks when dry; well suited for smoking: adds flavour, smells good.

Cherry: good for smoking and grilling; adds flavour. Gather after pruning or pick up wild cherry branches.

Fir: burns quickly, gives off a lot of heat and light; embers emit sparks, but fewer than spruce; not suitable for smoking.

Horse chestnut: not very suitable for burning, produces a lot of sparks.

Larch: burns easily; lively bright flames, few embers, lots of sparks.

Lime: easily flammable, good to start a fire with, but produces little heat; pleasant flames.

Maple: produces good hot flames for cooking and good embers.

Oak: difficult to light, burns slowly, hot and long lasting; gives excellent embers, not very bright flames.

Pine: burns easily, brightly and vividly; strong soot production due to high resin content; forms few embers emit sparks.

Poplar: easy to light, good to start a fire with but does not give off much heat; gives a bright light.

Spruce: easily flammable, easy to light, but not suitable for smoking: makes the food taste oily; forms embers quickly, but very few, and emits a lot of sparks.

White beech: very high burning quality – long lasting, hot and slow; few sparks, pleasant and bright flames.

Willow: does not burn very well; gives hardly any embers; very little smoke.

METHODS OF COOKING ON AN OPEN FIRE

'A man is rich in proportion to the number of things he can afford to let alone.'
Henry David Thoreau

Despite all the expensive high-tech barbecues, electronic grills and other equipment available for grilling and smoking, the joy of eating is best experienced at a simple open fire. With the traditional cooking methods of the outdoor kitchen we can experience anew the beauty of simple things and stimulate our creativity. The art of outdoor cooking lies in creating plain as well as elaborate dishes with the simplest resources. The most important ingredients are imagination, a spirit of improvisation, creativity and a pinch of time. In this book you will find recipes for all the following cooking methods.

Cooking in embers and ashes
This way of cooking is probably the most ancient. You can prepare many dishes in the embers of a fire or, for some recipes, in the hot ashes. You can cook not only vegetables such as potatoes, peppers, aubergines or artichokes but also eggs, chestnuts, flatbread or meat in the embers or the hot ashes.

To give enough embers for cooking a fire will need to burn for at least two hours. The white ash that forms on the embers serves as an insulating layer for food that needs less heat. Certain foods can be cooked directly in the embers without insulation, as for example Chicken Wrapped in Clay (page 63). To cook vegetables gently, push the embers aside, put the vegetables on the hot ground and cover them with hot ashes. Sometimes you can just cook at the edge of the bed of embers, as for example when cooking in a bottle or on a board.

Recipes: Baba Ghanoush, page 94; Chocolate Bananas, page 74; Corn Cobs in the Embers, page 127; Chapatti, page 185; Chicken Wrapped in Clay, page 59

Cooking on embers with clay
With this method, you wrap meat or vegetables in clay and place them in the embers. The clay hardens in the heat and the food cooks in its own juice, which makes it tender and aromatic. Instead of using clay, you can also wrap the food in salt dough.

Recipes: Chicken Wrapped in Clay, page 59; Filled Chicken in Salt Dough, page 56

Cooking on a flat stone

A flat stone makes an ideal hotplate, grill or baking surface. Put it into the embers or on stones above the fire and heat it for about an hour. Then sweep off the ashes with a twig and, if necessary for what you would like to cook or bake, grease the stone. Now you can grill vegetables, or meat or fish on skewers, bake bread and cakes, or roast acorns and other nuts on it.

Instead of a flat stone you can also use a roof tile or a washed concrete slab.

Caution: do not use wet or damp stones, as they can easily crack and cause injuries.

Recipes: Egg in Bread, page 128; Acorn Flatbread, page 140; Root Crisps, page 139

Cooking in a leaf

Instead of aluminium foil you can cook meat and vegetables wrapped in large fresh leaves from wild plants such as burdock, coltsfoot or butterbur. You can also wrap bread or biscuit dough in leaves and bake them on a hot stone. Meat and vegetables can be wrapped in leaves for cooking in an earth pit (see below).

Recipes: Feta Cheese in a Coltsfoot Leaf, page 34; Cookies in a Leaf, page 116; Meat and Vegetables in an Earth Oven, page 98

Ember pit

For this you need to dig a hole in the ground 20–30 cm/8–12 inches deep; the width depends on the amount of food you wish to cook in the pit. Light a fire in the pit and keep it burning for 1–2 hours until a bed of embers 10–15 cm/4–6 inches deep bed has formed. Do not add more wood at this point. The heat of the embers accumulates in the pit and cooks the food indirectly. Fix pieces of fish or meat on a board and put it at the edge of the ember pit: they will cook as in an oven. You can also bake bread or cakes by putting them next to the embers in a flat wide pan.

Recipes: Salmon on a Board, page 85

Earth pit or oven

Our ancestors used to prepare entire pigs, goats or large fish in earth pits and to this day many primitive tribes use this cooking method. In Hawaii an earth oven is called imu; the Maoris call it umu; on the Fiji Islands they call it lovo, in Mexico barbacoa and in Peru pachamanca.

To make an earth oven, dig a pit about 50 cm/18 inches deep, and sufficiently wide for the amount of meat you plan to cook, and line it with stones. Light a fire in the pit and keep it burning for about 2 hours. When the fire has burned down, cover it with a layer of fresh grass and lay the meat and vegetables – wrapped in leaves or placed in a pot or roaster – on top. Cover them with another layer of grass and then fill up the pit with earth and hot stones. Light a fire on top of the pit and let it burn for 1–1½ hours. Open the pit after 2–3 hours (depending on the size of the wrapped food) and take out the cooked food. Depending on the type and amount of food, cooking time needed can be from 1 hour (fish) to several hours (larger pieces of meat). It takes some experience to choose the right time to open the earth pit.

Cooking in an earth oven is a real celebration anywhere in the world. It is associated with hospitality and social gatherings. So, invite your 'clan' – family and friends – to join you. This is true adventure cooking.

Recipes: Venison in an Earth Oven, page 157; Vegetables and Meat in an Earth Oven, page 104; Venison in a Pot in an Earth Pit, page 156

Ember stones

Our prehistoric ancestors, who had no metal pots and pans, were quite resourceful and invented the animal-skin pot for making a warming soup or hearty stew in the cold of the Ice Age. They dug a pit in the ground and coated it with animal skins (fur side down) and weighted it down with stones on the edges. They filled this skin pot with water, meat, wild plants, berries, etc. Then they cooked it by adding glowing hot stones previously heated in a fire.

It is amazing how fast you can cook a vegetable soup or herbal tea with ember stones. Using the same method, you can also cook in birch bark bowls. Fill the bowls with finely chopped vegetables, meat and water. Add small stones heated in the fire and mix well. Repeat with further stones until everything is cooked.

You can even heat water in a paper cup by this method: fill the cup with water and add hot stones. You can make herbal tea or boil an egg, or boil water for drinking, in this way. Paper cups can stand temperatures of up to 200C°/392°F and boiling water in normal air pressure never reaches more than 100C°/212°F. Try it.

A variation of ember stone cooking, still practised in Mongolia, is khorkhog: meat stew with hot stones. Fill a large metal milk churn with layers of hot fist-sized stones, lightly salted pieces of mutton and vegetables. Then pour a little water into the bottom of the churn, close the lid with a metal clasp and put it in a hot oven. The meat and vegetables are cooked slowly with heat from all sides.

Recipe: Stone Age Soup, page 50

Ember burning

Ember burning is a good way of making a container out of wood. Cut a thick log or branch in half lengthwise and put a glowing ember on the flat surface. Holding the ember in place with a small twig, keep blowing on it while the heat eats its way into the wood, creating a hollow. As soon as the embers have charred the first layer of wood, scratch it out with a twig. Continue working in this way until the piece of wood is hollowed as desired. Keep renewing the embers. Finally, scrape out the hollow with a sharp stone and polish the cavity with sand and water. With this method you can also make wooden spoons and ladles out of logs or branches.

Recipe: Stone Age Soup, page 46

Clay pot

Since the Neolithic Age, people have been cooking with clay pots that they have fired themselves. An example of this age-old tradition is the clay baker, which has experienced many a renaissance in our kitchen, or the tagine, the traditional Moroccan clay pot. Cooking in a clay pot requires some experience, as great differences in temperature can cause the pots to crack or break.

A modern clay pot with a lid, the so-called pot au feu, can be used on an open fire as well as on your stove at home, for boiling, baking and roasting. Cooking this way is a healthy cooking method which requires little fat and conserves the flavour of the food very well.

Firing drinking bowls or cooking pots yourself is a special experience that gives you a taste of living in the Neolithic Age. Read about it in a specialist book or visit a workshop on the subject. You can see a self-made clay pot on page 147.

Recipes: Venison Stew, page 146; Power Breakfast, page 129

Skewers

Nature offers plenty of material for skewers. Green branches from deciduous trees such as ash, hazel, willow or maple are ideal. Fresh wood from conifer trees can give food an oily, bitter taste and is therefore not so good. Soak dry branches in water before using them when grilling so that they will not burn. Stick long skewers into the ground diagonally next to the fireplace and lay shorter ones across the stones around the fireplace or grill them on hot stones, a muurikka (see page 22) or a metal slab.

If you use the woody stems of rosemary, mugwort, lavender or sage, they will give grilled food an additional herbal flavour.

Caution: do not use skewers from poisonous trees and bushes such as yew, thuja, spindle, mezereon, cherry laurel, oleander or laburnum.

Skewers are ideal for quick-cooking foods such as poultry, tofu, mushrooms, bread and fish.

Recipes: Chicken Satay, page 110; Bread on a Stick, page 183; Fish on a Stick, page 78; Crostini, page 137; Tofu Skewers, page 37

Grill

The basic rule is: grill only above embers, not above flames. It is only worth getting a cast iron grill if you will use it a lot; otherwise you can convert a metal doormat into a grill. When you are on the move, a light grill is better. In outdoor shops you can get mini grills that easily fit into a rucksack or bag. When you cook meat or sausages on a grill, meat juices and fat drip into the embers, producing cancer-producing chemicals; a healthy alternative is to grill next to instead of above the embers, where the food will be cooked with radiant heat.

Recipe: Salmon on a Board, page 85

You can also use fresh twigs to make a grilling rack (for example, for fish), or to make a snowshoe grill.

Recipes: Grilled Fish in a Wicker Grillmesh, page 81; Salmon on a Snowshoe Grill, page 87

Wicker mesh

To steam meat, vegetables or dumplings, set a mesh made of flexible wicker or hazel sticks in a pot and lay the food on it. Then pour a little water into the pot and heat it up. This will produce steam. Adding herbs such as thyme, rosemary or sage to the water will give the food additional flavour.

If you put a wicker mesh in a tin can, you will have a smoke box in which you can smoke cheese, meat, fish, tofu or salt (in a cloth).

Recipes: Momos, pages 100–1; Smoked Cheese, page 104

Pots, roasters and pans

Choose your pots and pans according to weight and purpose. Look for them at flea markets or second-hand shops.

Large enamel pots, as used in the past for making preserves, are ideal for cooking on an open fire, for preparing stews for large groups or for baking a large loaf of bread. Enamel roasters are excellent for cooking roasts or poultry in an earth pit. Thanks to the smooth surface, enamel dishes are easy to clean, non-stick and acid- and temperature-resistant. But do not use steel wool or scrubbing sponges to clean them. The only disadvantage of enamel is that the enamel layer can crack upon strong impact and flake off.

Aluminium pots are particularly light and therefore ideal for outdoor cooking. They can, however, melt when exposed to great heat above embers. A more expensive but more heat-resistant alternative is two-

layered pots made of stainless steel and aluminium, or ultra-light titanium.

Cast iron pots and pans are traditionally used for cooking on an open fire or a wood-burning stove. Cast iron material retains the heat for longer and distributes it evenly. Cast iron cookware should be seasoned before first use. Rinse with hot water, dry thoroughly and rub with cooking oil. Then bake in the oven at 180°C/350°F/gas mark 4 for 1 hour. Wash them with hot water only, never with washing-up liquid, abrasive cleansers or pan scourers.

You can find Italian maroni pans (chestnut pans) in cookware shops or on the Internet.

Some food and drinks, such as polenta in Italy, Feuerzangenbowle (a rum punch) in Germany or bouillabaisse (a French fish soup) are traditionally prepared in copper kettles. Copper pots are lighter than cast iron ones, and you can flatten any dents quite easily yourself. However, copper cookware requires a lot of care and is suited for outdoor use only to a limited extent.

The following rule applies to all pots and pans for the open fire: they should not have synthetic handles or attachments. A non-stick coating is also not advisable. Pans for outdoor use are available with fold-up handles. It is advisable to get fireproof gloves for handling hot pots and pans on the fire (available from DIY shops).

Recipes: the Large Loaf, page 154; Venison in a pot in an Earth Pit, page 149; Chestnuts in a Chestnut Pan, page 152

Pot stands
There are various possibilities for placing pots over the fire or in the embers:
- Stones: put similar-sized stones around the fire or embers and place the cookware on top. Bricks are ideal.
- Grill: the bigger the pot, the stronger the grill has to be.
- Tripod: a metal tripod is good for hanging pots above embers or low flames.
- Wooden constructions: you can hang pots with handles on a forked branch rammed into the ground at an angle next to the fire. You can also make your own tripod out of strong branches: stand three branches together and tie them together at the top with string or wire. Or place a forked branch on either side of the fire and lay a strong branch across them.

Jugs
For an authentic cowboy breakfast, a metal or enamel jug is a must. I discovered these jugs in the desert camps of the Bedouins. They are available in camping supply shops. I bought my large jug for the campfire at a market in Egypt.

Dutch oven

With a Dutch oven you can confidently prepare on an open fire any dish for which you would normally require a kitchen oven. This piece of cooking equipment, still popular in the USA, accompanied the first European settlers on their covered-wagon treks across the continent.

The Dutch oven is a solid cast-iron cooking pot that is very stable thanks to its three metal legs. Dutch ovens are available in various sizes. The heavy lid lets no steam escape, allowing the food to simmer in its own juices and optimally retaining the flavour of soups and stews. Cast iron stores heat for a long time and distributes it evenly on the inside of the oven. A trademark of the Dutch oven is the high rim on the lid, which provides room to place embers on the top to create a kind of oven with upper heat; this is ideal for baking pizza, tarte flambée and bread, for boiling and for much more. You will need a lid-lifter, since the lid gets very hot. Thanks to its high rim, the lid can be also used as a pan. There are exact instructions on the amount of embers you require for each dish when using the Dutch oven with charcoal: be sure to follow these. When you use it with embers you have produced yourself in a campfire, you will have to learn by experience. Try it out, and do not despair if your first cakes or pizzas do not turn out as they should.

In time the Dutch oven will acquire a patina, a coating of fat on top of the initial coating from the seasoning, protecting it from corrosion. Clean it with hot water only, never with steel wool or scrubbing sponges.

Because of the weight of a Dutch oven, it is not particularly suitable for hikes. On camping trips in the car, mobile home or canoe, however, it is the best piece of equipment for your outdoor kitchen.

Recipes: Tartes Flambées, page 191; Colourful Pizza, page 142; Pizza with Dandelions, page 142

Hobo oven

This handy piece of cookware was developed by the hobos, the North American migratory workers commemorated in Jack London's books and to this day surrounded by an aura of glamour and adventure. They used as an oven a simple metal barrel in which they stabbed holes just above the bottom. Above these, they cut out an opening that

served as a door, so that they could light a fire in the bottom of the barrel. Just below the top of the barrel, which was closed with a lid, they cut out two more holes to allow the smoke to escape. When they lit a fire in the bottom of the barrel, the lid heated up so that food could be fried on it. In addition, the barrel served as a heater. If the barrel had no lid, they simply placed a large pot over the opening.

A hobo oven is more efficient than a gas cooker, as it works like a kind of chimney. It is amazing how little wood you need to prepare food on one. A few twigs and dry leaves will do – and your coffee or soup will be steaming hot.

You can make your own hobo oven out of a metal barrel or tin of any size. Nowadays you can buy small, light hobo ovens that are particularly suitable for hikes. If the oven has a metal bottom, you can light a fire where it would normally not be possible to do so directly on the ground.

Recipe: Chicken Satay, page 116

Muurikka

This large almost-flat rimless pan with handles comes from Finland. It is slightly curved, a bit like a wok. The muurikka can be suspended above a fire on a tripod, or placed on stones directly over the fire. It requires more wood than a hobo oven. The muurikka is very versatile: you can bake pancakes or flatbread in it, or use it to grill sausages, meat, fish and food on skewers; you can also prepare vegetable, meat or rice dishes such as paella for a large group of people with it. With this

cooking method, the fat cannot drip into the fire and cause carcinogenic hydrocarbons.

Tagine

A tagine is a Moroccan clay pot available in various sizes. You can put it on a pot stand above the embers, or on a special tagine oven filled with charcoal. The latter can be used in places where a fire would be prohibited or not possible, such as a terrace or balcony. The clay of the tagine distributes the heat slowly, leaving your food juicy and full of flavour. You do not open the tagine or stir the food during the cooking process, so you have time to relax by the fire or the oven.

The tagine has to be seasoned before you use it for the first time. Soak it in water for 3 hours, dry and rub it with vegetable oil; then put it in the oven at 200°C/400°F/gas mark 6 for 20 minutes. Before each use you must soak the tagine for 30 minutes and grease the bottom with oil. After several uses the soaking time can be reduced. Each time, the pores of the clay close more and more, as a patina forms and acts like a natural glaze. After regular use for a longer period, the tagine no longer has to be soaked. Keep it in a dry and airy place. A tagine cracks easily and is quite heavy, so it is not very suitable for cooking on hikes. But if you are travelling by canoe, car or caravan, you can create a sociable atmosphere with it and prepare delicious dishes in it.

Pressure cooker

You can easily convert a simple pot with a lid into a pressure cooker. Knead some flour and water together into a smooth dough and roll it into a strip

so that it fits around the outside of the pot. Firmly press the dough around the seam between the pot and the lid (the lid should not protrude). This way you seal the pot. When you put the pot over a fire, the dough hardens with the heat and the aroma stays inside the pot. This method is ideal for stews and cooking in hay.

Recipes: Vegetables on a Bed of Hay, page 103; Lamb on a Bed of Hay, page 102

Metal fire pit

Wherever you are not able or allowed to make a fire directly on the ground – for instance on a lawn, on a terrace, by tree roots or in a residential area – you can use a metal fire pit. Metal fire pits are available in DIY shops. You can use a grill to put your pots and pans over the fire or the embers in the pit.

Swedish log fire

Swedish or Finnish log fires are an excellent light source at parties. You can also put pots or jugs on one of these and use the fire for cooking at the same time.

To make a Swedish log fire, cut a piece of wood from a branch or tree trunk with a diameter of 20–30 cm/8–12 inches (see photograph), and with a handsaw or chainsaw cut a cross into it to about halfway down. Stand it upright. Put a firelighter or a piece of cloth soaked in petroleum in the crack, and light it. The fire will slowly eat its way into the wood and produce a wonderful light at night. Swedish log fires, also called tree torches, are available in DIY shops.

Cooking in bottles

Fireproof bottles and glass containers are ideal for cooking stews such as ratatouille, or for steaming vegetables. Place the bottles filled with the ingredients at the edge of the embers of a fire. It is a good idea to put a stone behind the bottle as a heat reflector. Strong heat fluctuation can cause the bottles to burst and you should therefore wrap the bottles in aluminium foil. Caution: never seal glasses or bottles, as they can explode.

Recipes: Ratatouille, page 40; Asparagus in a Bottle, page 41; Fagioli al Fiasco, page 38

Clay oven

Building a clay oven, as our ancestors did in the Neolithic Age, is an exciting experience, especially in your own garden or as a creative activity with children. You can build one out of natural materials from around you – clay, wicker branches and straw. And when you take out your first pizza, the project will really have been worthwhile. To build a clay oven, refer to a specialist book or go to a workshop on the subject.

THE ART OF IMPROVISATION

'"Men have no more time to understand anything. They buy things all ready made at the shops," said the fox to the little prince.'
Antoine de Saint-Exupéry

Cooking on an open fire stimulates your creativity, your imagination and your talent for improvisation – it allows you to discover and try out unusual cooking methods such as cooking in leaves, tree bark, coconut shells, tin cans, canvas or paper cups. For instance, you can fill a paper cup or a pot made of tree bark with water, tea, coffee or soup and put it in the hot ashes or on a grill. Australian settlers used to make their legendary billy tea in metal cans with wire handles – with a few eucalyptus leaves added perhaps. If, with all the things you find in the countryside, you ask yourself: 'What can I make out of this? What can I use it for?', you will quickly have a fully equipped outdoor kitchen. By shaping through ember burning, a curved branch becomes a ladle. A split branch of pine or fir becomes a practical whisk. A large piece of tree bark serves as a cooking pot, serving platter or surface for rolling out dough. A large leaf, such as one of butterbur or burdock, could be a plate, a lid, a container or even a rain hat. Because of the fine crystals on its leaves, snake grass (horsetail), together with sand and water, makes an excellent scouring pad with which to clean pots. The ash from the fire gets rid of grease on dishes. If you get resin on your hands, just remove it with some squashed rowan berries or barberries. Poplar fluff works well as a stopper in bottles used for cooking. You can make the finest colander ever out of wicker twigs and cleavers (catchweed). A fist-sized river pebble and a flat stone will make a practical food processor for cracking nuts, making pesto with wild herbs or crushing acorns. The white ash from a fire can be a substitute for baking powder.

By melting resin in a tin on the embers, you can easily produce a versatile 'Stone Age glue' which you can also use to seal cracks in wood. Or you can use melted resin to fix a sharp stone (especially a flint) into a crack in a piece of wood, to make a wonderful kitchen knife. Stalks of grass, bound together, make an efficient pastry brush, which you can also use to grease a hot waffle iron.

As mentioned earlier you can make a steamer with which to cook vegetables, meat or dumplings by wedging fresh flexible branches into the bottom of a cooking pot; fresh branches can also be used to make a grill or a snowshoe grill with which to cook fish. There is a wide selection of natural drinking straws, which you may sometimes find not even very far from your fireplace.

All these discoveries and many more will make you feel all the more at ease in the countryside, as you realize that you have everything you need at hand.

WILD PLANTS FOR THE OUTDOOR KITCHEN

When we cook on a campfire, nature's herb garden is often just a few steps away. It offers us a wide range of rich and valuable plants that we can use as flavourings, in vegetable dishes and salads, as teas, fillings and drinks and much more. Wild herbs and vegetables often contain up to twice the amount of vitamins and minerals as cultivated vegetables. They are full of vitalizing, original and wild energy. Dandelions, gallant soldiers (*Galinsoga*) and nettles, for instance, have a far higher iron content than their domesticated siblings. These 'power vegetables' therefore give dishes cooked outdoors not only an intense flavour and a unique touch but also high nutritional value. Used correctly, they can convert the simplest dish into a gourmet experience.

Wild herbs are wonderful gifts from nature, which we should treat with great respect so that they do not become extinct because of over-harvesting.

Gather with care

Gather plants only where there are enough, and take only as much as you need. When you make yourself at home outdoors, care for the countryside as you would your own garden: pick up litter and help protect rare and endangered plants.

Where to gather

Pick plants only in clean places where there are no pesticides from farms. Do not gather plants next to roads, motorways or railway embankments. Plants that grow there contain high levels of heavy metals and other harmful substances. Do not pick plants in nature reserves.

What to gather

Do not pick any protected plants. Gather only plants you can identify with certainty. If you are inexperienced, pick only familiar plants such as dandelions, nettles and daisies. You can extend your knowledge about plants little by little on guided hiking tours and courses, and by consulting specialist literature.

Here is a selection of common plants you can use for cooking.

Wild plants to use for vegetables, salads, fillings, stews and deep frying

Leaves: nettles, Good King Henry, meadow salsify, cabbage thistle, wild garlic, sorrel, daisies, garlic mustard, watercress, cuckoo flower, ground elder, chickweed, comfrey, coltsfoot, gallant soldiers, dandelion
Roots: wild garlic, silverweed, evening primrose, burdock, dandelion
Stems: burdock, common hogweed, garden angelica, spike primrose
Hop shoots
Buds: wild garlic, meadow salsify

Wild plants for seasoning

Leaves: thyme, marjoram, meadow sage, horseradish, wild mustard leaves – and flowers, mint, ground ivy, mugwort and garlic mustard
Seeds: caraway, garden angelica, hogweed, nettles, sorrel
Roots: common polypody, avens, water avens
Juniper berries

Wild berries for cooking
Fresh berries for muesli, cakes, pancakes and angelica boats: woodland strawberries, brambles, raspberries, blueberries, red currants, lingonberries

Fresh berries for compote, jam, desserts, game dishes, deep-fried cheese, acorn flatbread, dulce de leche: barberries, cornelian cherries, elderberries, lingonberries, wild cherries, rose hips, sarvis berries, rowan berries

Fresh berries for fruit soups: elderberries, cornelian cherries, wild cherries, sloes, rosehips
Tips: add the roots of avens, which give soup a clove aroma; meadowsweet flowers make for a subtle vanilla flavour; marjoram flowers add a spicy note

Fresh or dried fruits and berries for fruit teas: wild apple slices, barberries, woodland strawberries, rose hips, cornelian cherries, buckthorn berries, sarvis berries

Nuts and seeds for baking and roasting
Beechnuts, walnuts, hazelnuts, maple seeds, acorns, nettle seeds, sorrel seeds, Himalayan balsam seeds

Herbs for cooking with hay
Yellow sweet clover, white clover flowers, woodruff, sweet grass, elderflowers, meadow sage, thyme, marjoram, mugwort, St John's wort, meadowsweet flowers

Wild plants for the best herbal teas
Leaves: mint, yellow sweet clover, wild red currants
Blossoms: meadowsweet, daisies, pineapple weed, violets, wild roses, lime tree, elderflowers, red clover, sloe, acacia
Also: poplar buds, dried woodland strawberries, rose hips, dried wild apple slices, needles and twigs of Douglas fir, pine tree, silver fir and larch

BAKING BREAD ON THE FIRE

On a longer hike, far from any shops, or on a longer canoeing trip, we sometimes long for a piece of fresh bread. In moments like these, baking your own bread is a special experience that will make you feel at home and comfortable, no matter where you are. You need only flour, water and a pinch of salt to make flatbread in the hot ashes of a fire or Indian flatbread on a hot stone. You can easily refine these into small cakes or rolls with honey, nuts or wild fruits, and then bake them on a hot stone or under a pot. And if you happen to have some dry yeast with you, you can even satisfy your craving with a nice big loaf of bread.

I fondly remember the freshly baked bannock we used to enjoy on cold windy mornings on a canoeing trip in the north of Canada, and the big steaming loaf we made on the bank of an enchanted lake in Scandinavia – eaten just with butter, this was a real delicacy. It never ceases to amaze the participants of my wilderness seminars when we serve focaccia or Lebanese flatbread from the open fire. I am always delighted by children's enthusiasm when they bake bread on a stick, flatbread on a hot stone or cookies in a leaf, on one of the Stone Age courses I lead.

Whichever cooking utensils you have at your disposal, you can bake bread any time anywhere. You can find recipes for the following in this book (see index):

In hot ashes: ash flatbread

On a skewer: bread on a stick

On a hot stone or roof tile: oak flatbread, flatbread, chapatti, poppadoms

In a pan: pancakes, bannock, focaccia, poppadoms, chapatti, flatbread in an ember pit

In a pot: large loaf (with a second pot), smaller loaves, rolls

In a Dutch oven: bread loaf (possible without a second pot), flatbread, Lebanese flatbread, chapatti, pancakes, poppadoms

In a hobo oven: bread loaf (with a second pot)

In a tagine: flatbread, focaccia, Lebanese flatbread, chapatti, pancakes

In a muurikka: flatbread, chapatti, pancakes, bannocks

In a clay oven: bread, rolls, flatbread

SPRING

Nature has awakened, and is full of sensuous surprises. The mild, velvety air bears the scent of warm earth and blossom. The first migrating birds have returned. You have a sudden urge to be out in the open, sitting under trees in full bloom and feasting at an open fire.

FETA CHEESE IN A COLTSFOOT LEAF
Something tasty – well wrapped

In the cooking cultures of many countries food is wrapped in leaves for cooking – for instance in the Caribbean and in South America banana leaves are used. This method is especially practical for cooking fish, which is marinated with oil, salt and spices, wrapped in a leaf and slowly cooked on the grill. Feta cheese, too, tastes incomparably good when cooked in a leaf.

Serves 4

200 g (7 oz) 1 cup feta cheese

4 fresh coltsfoot leaves

freshly gathered herbs such as thyme, marjoram, meadow sage, juniper berries and wild garlic bulbs or kitchen herbs such as rosemary, basil, tarragon, hyssop, spring onions and garlic

Cut the feta into flat rectangles, not too thick. Place one piece on one half of each coltsfoot leaf. Spread the herbs on both sides of the cheese. Wrap the other half of the leaf around the cheese and fix with a small wooden skewer or tie together with the stem.
Put on a grilling rack and cook above the embers for about 20 minutes until the cheese is soft and can be spooned out of the leaf.

This goes wonderfully with toasted bread, ash loaf or focaccia.

Tip
You can also use a mild aromatic goat cheese. Sprinkle pepper and herbs such as thyme, marjoram and lavender flowers on the cheese. Drizzle with oil and wrap in the leaf. Do not turn over the packages during grilling, so that the cheese does not leak.

Variations
Put some pepperoni on the cheese or roll it in sesame or roasted nettle seeds before grilling.

Cooking utensils
Grill (a clay oven or Dutch oven are also an option); 4 small wooden skewers carved out of branches and sharpened.

Fire
Fire with a good bed of embers.

Wild plant information
Instead of the coltsfoot leaf in other seasons you can use burdock of butterbur leaves. Caution: do not use giant hogweed leaves as there is danger of allergies upon contact with the plant and direct sunlight.

TOFU SKEWERS
Vegetarian Finger Food

Tofu is made from soybeans. It has no natural flavour and is therefore usually marinated in soy sauce or another marinade before cooking. With smoked tofu this is not necessary, as it already has a hearty flavour.

For 6–8 skewers

200 g (7 oz) 1 cup smoked tofu (available from health food or Asian shops)

6–8 button mushrooms

1 red pepper

8–10 cherry tomatoes

salt, pepper

Cut the smoked tofu into cubes. Leave smaller mushrooms whole and cut bigger ones in half. Halve the pepper, remove the seeds and cut into bite-sized pieces. Alternate the vegetables and the tofu on skewers, leaving the ends free. Grill for 15–20 minutes. Season with salt and pepper or barbecue sauce.

Variations
Other possibilities to cook on skewers: pieces of onion, olives, artichoke hearts, courgette slices, pre-boiled potatoes, pieces of broccoli, peperoncini (mild peppers of chillies), aubergines, fruit such as bananas, pineapple, etc.

Tips
If you soak the skewers in water for about 20 minutes they will not burn. Instead of tofu you can use halloumi. Marinate in olive oil and herbs before grilling. It is also possible to cook this on a muurikka.

Cooking utensils
6–8 skewers (e.g. carved out of thin, green, firm twigs); grill laid across two stones above the embers, or a muurikka.

Fire
Mature bed of embers without flames.

Marinade:

100 ml/½ cup soy sauce

1 piece fresh ginger (about 2 cm/¾ inches) peeled and finely chopped

juice of 1 lemon

1 tbsp finely chopped wild herbs, e.g. mint, wild garlic, wild mustard

200 g (7 oz) 1 cup tofu

2–3 tbsp sesame seeds

Variation: with unsmoked tofu
Make a marinade with all the marinade ingredients. Dice the tofu and leave in the marinade for 20–30 minutes. Meanwhile roast the sesame seeds in a dry pan for about 2 minutes until golden brown. Roll the marinated tofu in the sesame seeds, put on skewers and grill for 2–5 minutes over the embers.

Caution
Make sure you do not confuse wild garlic with lily-of-the-valley. The leaves look exactly the same; the only difference is that the wild garlic leaves have a strong garlic smell and the lily-of-the-valley leaves smell like flowers.

FAGIOLI AL FIASCO
Beans in a bottle

This traditional method is probably the best way to cook beans. It comes from Tuscany and is a speciality of the city of Florence, where beans are prepared in a round-bodied bottle or demijohn (called a fiasco; if the bottle is sealed firmly with a cork during the cooking process, it can burst and that would indeed be a fiasco). Traditionally, in the evening the beans in the bottle were placed in the warm embers, or in a wood stove after bread-baking, and by morning they were cooked.

Serves 2–3

2 cups dried small white beans (e.g. cannellini)

2 garlic cloves or 4 fresh wild garlic cloves

1 sprig of sage or about 6 fresh garden or meadow sage leaves, (or dried sage leaves)

1 pinch pepper

50 ml/¼ cup extra virgin olive oil

water

½ tsp of salt

Soak the beans in water for about 10 hours and then drain. Put the beans into a bottle and add all the other ingredients except the salt. Fill the bottle three-quarters full with water and plug it with a kitchen towel or cotton wool. Wrap aluminium foil around the bottle and place the bottle at the edge of the campfire, close to the embers within the stones. The embers and the fire should not be too hot, as the beans should only simmer lightly; this is how the dish gets its incomparable smooth and aromatic flavour. Cook for 3 hours. The beans should remain covered with water during the entire cooking process. If too much water has evaporated, refill the bottle with warm water. (Caution: do not use cold water, as it causes the bottle to burst.) At the end of the cooking process, when all the water has evaporated, season with salt.

If you do not pre-soak the beans, the cooking process takes 9–10 hours. The beans taste even better that way.

This dish goes very well with grilled meat and fish. It also tastes very good with Italian salami, pecorino or just olives.

Caution

To reduce the risk of the bottle bursting, wrap it in aluminium foil (we did not do this in the photographs so that the content of the bottles is visible). If you use heat-resistant glass, or if the dish is prepared in a baking or clay oven, the aluminium foil will not be necessary.

Cooking utensils and fire

As for Asparagus in a Bottle, page 41.

RATATOUILLE
A colourful mix in a bottle

Serves 2–3

1 aubergine

1 red pepper

1 courgette

8 black olives, stoned, whole or chopped

1 tbsp chopped herbs

(e.g. oregano, rosemary, thyme, hyssop, tarragon)

2 bay leaves

2 garlic cloves, finely chopped

700–800 g (25–28 oz) 4⅓–5 cups peeled and chopped tomatoes (tin or glass)

½ litre (1 pint) 2 cups strained tomatoes

pepper, sea salt,

chilli powder (optional)

Dice the vegetables and together with the olives and the herbs put them into two wide-necked glass bottles. To each bottle add 1 bay leaf, 1 garlic clove and half the chopped and strained tomatoes, and season with salt and pepper and chilli powder if desired. The vegetables should just be covered by the liquid. Plug the bottle opening with a kitchen towel. Wrap the bottles in aluminium foil and put them close to the embers at the edge of the fire, and let the vegetables simmer lightly for 30–45 minutes until the vegetables are soft.

Tip

This goes very well with bread, pasta or couscous.

Basic recipe for couscous

In a pot, pour 350 ml (12 fl oz) 1½ cups of boiling vegetable stock on to 250 g (8 oz) 1½ cups of couscous and let it soak for about 5 minutes. Then loosen the couscous with a fork and squash any lumps. Add some butter (optional). Done!

Cooking utensils and fire

As for Asparagus in a Bottle, page 41.

Wild plant information

Once we cooked this dish on a fire in the mountains. We gathered mint, marjoram, wild thyme and wild chives and seasoned the ratatouille with those. It was delicious.

ASPARAGUS IN A BOTTLE
Gourmet veg in a bottle

Serves 2

5–8 thin white or green
asparagus spears
about ½ litre (1 pint) 2 cups water
(not too cold)
¼ untreated lemon, sliced
½ tsp sea salt, 1 tsp sugar

Cut off the tough ends of the asparagus spears. Put the asparagus in the bottle with the tip up. Add the water, lemon, salt and sugar. Plug the bottle opening with a cotton kitchen towel and put it close to the embers at the edge of the fire. Allow to simmer for 20–30 minutes until the asparagus is soft. Serve with melted butter or olive oil and lemon juice.

Tip

You can use the stock to make asparagus soup. Simply season it with salt and pepper, add cream and maybe thicken with some flour.

Cooking utensils

Wide-necked 1-litre (2 pint) glass bottle (e.g. a milk bottle or heat-resistant glass container); a cotton kitchen towel the size of a handkerchief or a piece of cotton wool (or gather poplar fluff and use that).

Fire

A mature fire with lots of embers and a corner where you can continue to burn wood so that you can shovel more embers towards the bottle. A keyhole fire is best here. Do not interrupt the cooking process.

Wild plant information

Young hop sprouts gathered in spring can also be cooked in a bottle in this way. Cooking time is 10 minutes maximum. Leaves of meadow salsify and peeled young stems of burdock are also suitable. They taste particularly good when served with olive oil, lemon juice and salt.

TEMPURA
Wild herbs in batter

Serves 4–6

Large individual leaves with stems, e.g. ground elder, chaparral, comfrey, nettles, individual large, but still young meadow sage leaves, garden sage (particularly tasty, an Italian speciality)

Batter:

250 g (½ lb) 2 cups flour

500 ml (1 pint) 2 cups water or milk

2 eggs

sea salt

a dash of beer (wheat beer is particularly suitable)

oil for deep-frying

pepper, curry powder (optional)

paprika, chilli powder

Blend all the ingredients for the batter together until smooth and of a relatively thin consistency. If necessary add more water. Heat plenty of oil in a pot or pan. Dip the individual leaves in the batter, remove any excess batter on the edge of the bowl and fry the leaves on both sides in the hot oil. Let any excess oil drip from the leaves before serving and season as desired.

Cooking utensils
A bowl; perhaps a whisk; a pot, pan or hobo oven.

Fire
Small fire with low flames.

On the move
Make the batter at home and take it with you.

Wild plant information
Blooming herb twigs are also suitable for this dish, e.g. yellow bedstraw, meadow sage, wild marjoram, wild carrot, wild parsnip, thyme.

COMFREY CORDON BLEU
A fine wild herb dish

Serves 3

1 portion beer batter
(see Tempura, page 42),
amount according to the
size of the comfrey leaves

6 palm-sized comfrey leaves
with stem, freshly picked

3 thin slices of cheese (e.g.
raclette cheese, Gruyère)

oil for deep-frying
(e.g. sunflower oil)

Prepare the batter. Place a slice of cheese between each pair of comfrey leaves. Press the leaves together at the edges. If they do not stick together, fix them with a small wooden stick. Dip both sides in the batter and deep-fry until golden brown.

This dish goes very well with lingonberry (cowberry), blueberry, rosehip or barberry purée, home-made from wild berries.

Variations
The filled comfrey leaves can also be breaded. Dip them in beaten egg and then cover in breadcrumbs. In addition to the cheese you can add ham to the filling.

Cooking utensils and fire
As for Tempura, page 42; also some thin wooden sticks or sharpened twigs to fix the leaves together if necessary.

NETTLE CHIPS
Nibbles for the wild

'Nettle chips – yuk, I don't like those!' is how the children of the wilderness groups I run react to the idea of this dish. But when they taste these crisps they cannot get enough of them and see nettles with new eyes.

Serves 3–4

125 g (4½ oz) ½ cup clarified butter or vegetable oil

1 bowl freshly picked individual nettle leaves, as young as possible (use gloves to pick them)

sea salt, cayenne pepper or paprika, salt

Heat the clarified butter or oil in a pan and fry the leaves in it, constantly stirring, until they are slightly curled and crispy. Take them out of the pan, allow the excess fat to drip off and sprinkle a mixture of salt and cayenne pepper or paprika on them. Serve hot.

Cooking utensils
A large flat pan; a board on which to let the excess fat drip off; a wooden spoon or fork for stirring and taking out the chips.

Fire
Small fire with low flames.

'Believe me, you will find something far greater in the woods than you will find in books. Stones and trees will teach you that which you will never learn from masters.'

Bernhard of Clairvaux

STONE AGE SOUP
Forget civilization

finely chopped leaves, e.g.:
cabbage thistle, Good King Henry,
chickweed, plantago, hogweed,
wild garlic

finely chopped roots e.g.:
burdock, silverweed,
couch grass, wild garlic

herbs such as large thyme,
oregano, wallpepper,
wild garlic bulbs, watercress

salt, pepper

water

1 pinch spirit of improvisation

Put the leaves, roots and herbs into the cooking container (see below) and cover with water. Take some glowing hot stones out of the embers with a long fork and place in the water, which will start to bubble and boil immediately. Repeat this two to three times until the ingredients are cooked and the soup is hot.

Variation
A slightly less Stone Age variation is to add vegetable stock. You can also add small pieces of jerky (see page 105) to the soup.

Cooking utensils
A home-made cooking bowl, e.g. a wooden bowl hollowed with embers (see page 17); a stone with a sizeable hollow or a container made of tree bark; small stones; long fork or tongs made of flexible branches.

Wild plant information
Some wild vegetables taste much more aromatic than their cultivated relatives. Wild vegetables also have a much higher nutritional value than cultivated vegetables. Hogweed leaves give the soup a subtle flavour of chicken stock (but see caution on page 34); plantago buds make artichokes go green with envy; chickweed is smoother and more aromatic than any spinach.

NINE HERBS SOUP
You must taste this soup, which is also called Green Soup or Maundy Thursday Soup.

Made with nine wild plants with especially powerful healing properties, it is considered to be a real 'power soup', strengthening the body with the powers of wild plants, especially in spring. The soup contains leaves of the following plants: nettles, ground ivy, dandelion, chickweed, sorrel, ground elder, ribwort plantain, daisies and yarrow.

For a Stone Age soup, boil the leaves in water and season with salt and pepper. For a more modern recipe, lightly braise some finely chopped onion in a little oil, add the finely chopped leaves and fill the pot with vegetable stock. Simmer lightly until the leaves are cooked. Add cream or crème fraîche to taste.

PIZZA CALZONE
Amazingingly simple

Calzone pizza pockets are ideal for a celebration or a party outdoors. Simply arrange the various ingredients on leaves as a buffet, so that each guest can create their own filling. I often make calzone pizza on my wildlife courses, and it is always a success and tastes delicious.

For 5–7 pizzas

1 packet natural dry yeast (from a health food shop) or ½ cube fresh yeast

500 g (1 lb) 3¾ cups flour

salt

2 tbsp of olive oil

about 200 ml (6¾ fl oz) ¾ cup water

Filling ingredients:

1–2 mozzarella balls or finely diced cheese

3 tomatoes, sliced

tinned tuna

salami, sliced

ham, sliced

pepperoni

herbs, e.g. basil, thyme, oregano (wild herbs are also good)

salt

Mix the dry yeast and the flour well; or completely dissolve the fresh yeast in some warm water or warm milk, and then add the flour. Add the salt, olive oil and water and knead into a smooth pizza dough. If the dough is too soft it may ooze through the grill. Form the dough into a ball, dust it with flour and leave to rest close to the fire for 1 hour in a bowl covered with a kitchen towel, until its volume has doubled.

Divide the dough into peach-sized balls and press flat. Put the desired filling ingredients on one half. Fold the other half over to form a half moon and press together thoroughly round the edges.

Place the filled pockets on the grill and bake above the embers for about 15 minutes, depending on the thickness of the dough. The calzone pizzas are done when you tap them and they sound slightly hollow. They can also be baked on a hot flat stone, clay oven or Dutch oven.

Tip
Instead of the tomato slices you can spread tomato purée or strained tomatoes on the dough before putting on the other ingredients.

Cooking utensils
A bowl; a grill with as little space possible between the bars or a flat stone.

Fire
A fire with a lot of mature embers and few flames.

Wild plant information
You can also fill the pizza pockets with wild herbs mixed with ricotta, quark or crème fraîche. Fresh thyme and wild marjoram give both variations an Italian flair. You can also season them with salt and pepper and perhaps nutmeg.

TABBOULEH
Wild-herb and couscous salad

Easy to prepare and ideal for a summer meal outdoors.

Serves 4

250 g (9 oz) 1½ cups couscous

350 ml (12 fl oz) 1½ cups vegetable stock

1 cucumber

2 tomatoes

1 cup freshly chopped wild herbs such as ground elder, mint, thyme, wild marjoram or alternatively 1 bunch flat-leaved parsley and ½ a bunch fresh mint

5 tbsp olive oil

the juice of ½ lemon

sea salt, pepper

2 pinches cumin

Put the couscous in a bowl. Pour in the boiling vegetable stock and leave to soak for 5 minutes. Then loosen up the couscous with a fork and squash any lumps. Peel and dice the cucumber, dice the tomatoes and add both to the couscous with the wild herbs.

Mix the olive oil, lemon juice, salt, pepper and cumin and stir into the couscous salad. Allow to marinate for about 10 minutes. If necessary add some seasoning.

This goes well with toasted bread, Lebanese flatbread and grilled meat. Baba Ghanoush (page 94) tastes particularly good with it. Peppermint tea optionally mixed with green tea and sweetened with sugar rounds off this dish Berber-style.

Tip
Instead of couscous you can use quinoa or bulgur wheat, pre-boiled in hot water.

Cooking utensils
A pot or hobo oven to boil water; a bowl.

Fire
A small fire with low flames.

BASY – COUSCOUS WITH VEGETABLES
A recipe from Senegal

This recipe is from Rokhaya N'diaye. I love her African cuisine, which she has brought us from Senegal. When I told her about this book she was not surprised and simply said: 'In Senegal everybody cooks on an open fire.' When I asked her to contribute a dish to the book, she arrived the same day with a bottle gourd, a pot and other utensils and cooked her Basy on the open fire. We ate it, according to tradition, with our hands out of one bowl – a technique that we didn't immediately master! It was delicious.

Serves 5–6

1 onion, finely chopped

2 garlic cloves, finely chopped

4 tbsp olive oil

1 red pepper, pitted and cut into large pieces

3 tomatoes, diced

3 courgettes, cut into thick slices

3 carrots, peeled and cut into thick slices

1 aubergine, diced

herbs such as rosemary, thyme, parsley, summer savory

1 litre (2 pints) 4 cups vegetable stock

Couscous:

500 g (17½ oz) 3 cups couscous

about 200 ml (6¾ fl oz) ¾ cup boiling water

½ tsp salt

2 tbsp olive oil

Lightly braise the onion and garlic in the olive oil, add the pepper and continue braising. Add the rest of the vegetables and the herbs, pour on the vegetable stock, bring to the boil and leave to simmer for 10 minutes.

Put the couscous in a bowl, pour on the boiling water, mix in the salt and olive oil and leave to soak for 5 minutes. Then mix the couscous with your hands to get rid of any lumps. Arrange the vegetables on top of the couscous.

Jniyde – bon appétit!

Tip
In Senegal this dish is traditionally served with hot green tea, which can also be made on the open fire.

Cooking utensils
A pot and a bowl.

Fire
A fire with low flames.

LEBANESE FLATBREAD
An oriental treat

I got this recipe from Juliette Leonore Delventhal, whose cuisine I enjoyed during a seminar in La Bolinas, California. She served this delicious flatbread on a long wooden table under a huge tree.

For about 10 loaves

Spice paste:

¾ cup dried chopped thyme leaves

1 tbsp sumac powder
(available in Turkish
or Middle Eastern
food shops)

2 tbsp sesame seeds, lightly
roasted in a pan without fat

1 tsp salt

1 tsp chilli powder

200 ml/1 cup best olive oil

1 small onion, very finely chopped

Dough:

1 packet natural dry yeast
(from a health food shop)
or ½ cube fresh yeast

about 500 ml (1 pint)
2 cups water

5 cups flour

50 ml/¼ cup olive oil

1 tsp salt

Mix all the ingredients for the spice paste in a small bowl or pot and leave to marinate.

To make the dough, mix the yeast with ¼ cup of water until smooth. Add 1 cup of flour and mix well. Then add the rest of the flour and water, and the oil and salt, and knead until the dough is smooth and no longer sticks to your hands. Form the dough into a ball and let it rise close to the fire for about 1 hour until its volume has doubled. Divide it into tangerine-size pieces and roll them out into ovals about 15 cm/6 inch long and 2–3 mm thick on a wooden board with flour. Cover them with a kitchen towel and let them rise for 10 minutes.

Put the dough pieces on a baking tray in a clay oven or on an upside-down pot on the floor of a Dutch oven. If you have no experience of baking flatbread, place them on greaseproof paper, or else they may burn slightly if you don't keep to the baking time exactly. Bake them at a high temperature (about 200°C/392 °F/gas mark 6) for about 5 minutes. They will inflate and form bubbles. As soon as they are slightly brown and crispy, take them out of the oven and spread the top with the spice paste. Serve hot.

The flatbread goes well with Baba Ghanoush (see page 94), Tabbouleh (see page 52) and grilled meat. The remaining spice paste can be kept in a glass screw-top jar in the fridge for 2–3 weeks.

Cooking utensils
A bowl; a small bowl; a rolling pin (e.g. a debarked branch); a board for rolling out the dough on; a Dutch oven or clay oven; a basting brush made of grasses tied together.

Fire
For a clay oven: pre-heat for about 1 hour. For a Dutch oven: mature fire with a lot of embers.

FILLED CHICKEN IN SALT DOUGH
Slow food, leisure food

1 chicken, kitchen-ready

2 lemons, unwaxed, sliced

Filling:

1 cup chopped herbs, fresh or dry,
such as rosemary, oregano, thyme,
sage, tarragon and/or wild herbs
such as ground ivy, thyme,
meadow sage, wild garlic

2 garlic cloves

2 tbsp olive oil

salt and pepper

Salt dough:

1 kg (2¼ lb) 7½ cups flour

500 g (1¼ lb) 2 cups salt

water

From the neck end, carefully separate the skin of the chicken from the meat. Push the lemon slices under the skin to prevent too much salt from seeping into the meat and drying it out. Chop the herbs or grind in a pestle and mortar, mix with the garlic, oil, salt and pepper and stuff into the cavity of the chicken.

Make a firm dough that does not stick to your hands out of the flour, salt and water. Roll it out to a thickness of about 1–2 cm/1 inch and cut in half. Put the chicken on to one half and cover it with the other half. Press the dough down firmly round the edges so that the chicken is in a completely sealed dough case. Wet any cracks in the dough with water or seal with another piece of dough. Put the chicken in the dough case into the embers and allow to cook for 2–3 hours. This way the chicken will cook in its own juice and the meat will be especially tender and juicy. Savour the appetizing aroma when you break open the dough case.

Variations
You can also prepare fish and other meat in this way.

Cooking utensils
A bowl or pot to make the dough; a rolling pin or thick branch to roll it out on; a board for rolling out the dough on.

Fire
A very mature fire that has been burning for at least 2 hours, with about 10 cm/4 inches of embers. The keyhole fireplace, in which you can constantly produce new embers, is ideal here. We prepared a chicken in this way in April in Tuscany, when the olive trees had just been pruned and the branches were being burned.

CHICKEN WRAPPED IN CLAY
A snug rooster

A chicken cooked in clay is also called a hobo chicken or Roma chicken. Travelling people such as the hobos (North American migratory workers) or the Roma people traditionally cooked their meat in this way, since it does not depend on a large dish; this allowed them to travel light yet be able to prepare a delicious dish anywhere where there was clay soil.

Cooking a chicken in clay is a fascinatingly primitive cooking method. The chicken is wrapped in clay soil and placed in the embers. When the clay ball is opened like a treasure chest, the cooked, golden-brown chicken emerges with a delicious aroma and juicy meat.

2 garlic cloves

2 tbsp Dijon mustard

3 tbsp extra virgin olive oil

6 tbsp chopped fresh or dried herbs such as thyme, rosemary and mint

pepper and sea salt

1 chicken, kitchen-ready

a few large leaves e.g. wild garlic, butterbur or long grass

about 2 kg (4½ lb) 9½ cups clay

Crush the garlic and make it into a paste with the mustard, oil, herbs and seasoning. Rub the paste into the outside of the chicken. Put the rest into the cavity of the chicken. Wrap the chicken in the large leaves or long grass and tie it up firmly with string.

Thoroughly knead the clay, removing any little stones, pieces of wood, etc. and pounding out air bubbles. Flatten the clay and wrap it around the chicken so that it is completely sealed. Fill any holes in the clay with more clay and some water.

Place the chicken wrapped in clay into the embers and cook for about 2–3 hours, depending on the size of the chicken. When the clay has dried on the surface, cover it with embers. Take the fired clay ball out of the embers and open it carefully, as hot steam will emerge.

Cooking utensils
About 2 kg (4½ lb) 9½ cups of clay; large leaves; string.

Fire
Mature fire with at least 10 cm/4 inches of embers.

Wild plant information
You can use other wild herbs to season the chicken: wild garlic bulbs, garlic mustard, oregano, watercress, mild mustard buds or cuckoo flower leaves; or wild berries, wild mushrooms and chestnuts.

RUSSIAN WOODCUTTERS' TREE CAKE
Sweets for tough men

This recipe comes from woodcutters in Eastern Europe. Batter and honey are layered around a tree trunk like annual rings to form a delicious tree cake.

300 g (10½ oz) 2⅓ cups flour

1 pinch salt

½–¾ litre (17–25 fl oz) 2–3 cups water

about 200 g (7 oz) ½ cup liquid honey (e.g. acacia honey)

In a bowl, mix the flour, salt and water into a thick but spreadable batter.

Debark a branch. From the centre of a keyhole fireplace, lay an ember trail of about 40 cm/16 inches and lay stones on either side of it as a support for the tree trunk. Lay the trunk on these so that it is about 10 cm/4 inches above the embers.

Spread the batter about 1–2 mm thick around the tree trunk and bake it above the embers, turning it until it is all golden brown. Then spread a thin layer of honey on top and allow it to caramelize slowly, still constantly turning the trunk. Then spread another layer of batter on top and bake that. Repeat this, alternating batter and honey up to about 10 layers. Cut the cake from the tree trunk and enjoy it while it is still warm.

Variation

Add some lemon zest or vanilla essence to the batter.

Tip

Instead of rolling the branch over the stones on either side of the ember trail you can fix two forked branches on either side of the embers and turn the tree trunk in those (as when grilling a chicken).

Cooking utensils

A debarked tree trunk or branch with a diameter of about 7 cm/3 inches and a length of about 60 cm/24 inches, depending on the width of the ember trail (lime and maple wood are especially suitable; do not use yew or thuja wood, as they are poisonous; oak and beech wood make the batter taste bitter); a bowl.

Fire

A keyhole fireplace with enough embers to make an ember trail.

BAUMSTRIEZEL
A fine pastry from Transylvania

Baumstriezel (tree cakes) actually look like tree trunks. Their origin is Transylvania, where they have been made since the end of the nineteenth century; they are known as kürtőskalacs in Hungary. Perhaps the Russian Woodcutters' Tree Cake (see page 60) is a precursor of the fine baumstriezel.

For 5–6 cakes

1 kg (2¼ lb) 7½ cups flour

1 pinch salt

2 cubes fresh yeast or the equivalent amount of dry yeast

2–3 tbsp sugar

about 500 ml (1 pint) 2 cups milk, slightly warmed

1 tsp vanilla seeds or vanilla essence

200 g (7 oz) 1 cup butter

2 eggs

For spreading on the outside:

6 tsp sugar (1 tsp per cake)

4 tbsp butter, melted

Put the flour into a bowl and mix with the salt. Make a well in the centre, crumble the yeast into it, add the sugar and mix with about 4 tbsp of warm milk. Cover and leave to rise for about 15 minutes. Then add the rest of the ingredients and knead into a smooth dough. Form a ball with the dough, cover and let it rise in a warm place for about 1 hour.

Meanwhile prepare the wooden stick (see below).

Divide the dough into 5–6 orange-sized portions and roll them into strips 70 cm/28 inches long and 1 cm/½ inch thick on a flat, firm surface. One by one, wind them around the greased wooden stick (perhaps having first covered the stick with aluminium foil to make it easier to remove the cakes later; the dough sticks less on maple wood). Lightly roll the stick with the dough on the work surface. Brush the cakes with melted butter and sprinkle with sugar.

Place the stick about a hand's breadth above the embers by laying it on bricks or flat stones on either side of the fire; or lay it across two forked branches. Bake the cakes for about 10 minutes, constantly turning them until the sugar has caramelized and they are golden brown. Then slide the cakes off the stick.

Tip
The delicious warm tree cakes go excellently with campfire coffee, hot chocolate or elderflower punch.

Variations
Sprinkle a mixture of sugar and cinnamon or sugar and ground walnuts or hazelnuts over the cakes. The dough can be varied by adding the zest of 1 lemon.

Cooking utensils

A bowl or pot for the dough; a wooden stick with handles; a small
pot in which to melt the butter and warm the milk; a work surface; a
pastry brush (e.g. made of grasses tied together); aluminium foil to
wrap around the stick (optional).

For the wooden stick: either take the handles out of a rolling pin and
insert branches about 50 cm/1½ ft long on both sides, or debark a
6-cm/2½ inch-thick branch without twigs (lime and maple wood are
especially suitable; do not use yew or thuja wood, as they are
poisonous; oak and beech wood make the batter taste bitter). Make
holes in both ends (e.g. with the tip of a knife) and insert two
handles. Wrap the wood in aluminium foil or grease with oil.

Fire

A fire with a good layer of embers and without flames; a keyhole
fireplace is ideal to comfortably bake 5–6 cakes.

GRANDMA'S WAFFLES
Pure bliss

This is the best way to make waffles. The hot waffle iron gives them a delicate caramel flavour and makes them soft and crispy at the same time. Quite simply, happiness is . . . Grandma's waffles.

For about 10 waffles
125 g (4½ oz) ½ cup butter
50 g (1¾ oz) ¼ cup sugar
1 pinch salt
4–5 eggs
250 g (½ lb) 2 cups flour
1 tsp baking powder
¼ litre (½ pint) 1 cup milk
sunflower oil to grease the waffle iron

Soften the butter by putting it in a bowl close to the fire and beat it with the sugar, salt and eggs until creamy. Gradually mix the flour, baking powder and milk into the batter, adding a spoonful at a time. Place a waffle iron above the embers on some bricks. It should be fixed high enough so that it can be turned. Heat the waffle iron and grease with oil. With a spoon or a ladle put some batter on one side of the waffle iron, spread it out and close the lid. After about 3 minutes turn the waffle iron and bake the other side for a few minutes. Take out the golden-brown waffles and allow to cool.

These waffles taste wonderful without anything. However, you can also sprinkle them with sugar and cinnamon or serve them with fruit compote.

Tip
There are many different types of waffle iron. I found my cast iron waffle iron (see photograph) at a jumble sale many years ago.

Cooking utensils
A waffle iron; a large spoon; a cup or ladle; a pastry brush made of grasses; if necessary a metal hook or a branch to turn your waffle iron.

Fire
A mature fire with a lot of embers. A keyhole fireplace is ideal, so that you can keep adding fresh embers under the waffle iron.

VANILLA WAFFLES
Especially tasty

For about 10 waffles

400 ml (13½ fl oz) 1½ cups water

100 g (3½ oz) ¾ cup powdered milk

200 g (7 oz) 1½ cups flour

1 tbsp honey

1 pinch salt

the seeds of 1 vanilla pod

2 eggs

1 tbsp vegetable oil (sunflower oil is especially good)

Put the water in a bowl. Add the powdered milk, flour, honey, salt and vanilla and leave to soak for 5 minutes. Add the eggs and oil and beat into a light batter. Bake the waffles in the waffle iron until golden brown. Enjoy them while they are warm.

Variations

Sprinkle with sugar and cinnamon or serve with maple syrup or hot berry compote. Briefly boil wild berries such as blueberries, elderberries, wild strawberries and wild cherries in a little water and sweeten to taste; or serve with wild berry purée from a jar (see page 140).

Cooking utensils

As for Grandma's Waffles, page 64.

Fire

A mature fire with a lot of embers – a keyhole fireplace is ideal.

ELFIN WAFFLES
Pretty as a picture

These wonderful waffles are like a work of art. They are also called wafer waffles. I call them elfin waffles, after an astonished child at the fire called out: 'But these are like waffles for elves!'

For about 16 waffles

2 eggs

50 g (1¾ oz) ¼ cup brown sugar

2 tbsp butter

1 tsp vanilla essence or vanilla seeds

1 tsp aniseed (fresh is best – e.g. aniseeds crushed between two stones)

350 g (12¼ oz) 1½ cups wholemeal flour (e.g. spelt)

100 ml (3⅓ fl oz) ½ cup sunflower oil

Beat the eggs and sugar in a bowl until creamy. Meanwhile, melt the butter close to the fire and whisk it into the sugar and egg mixture. Add the spices and the flour, mix and knead into a fairly firm dough that no longer sticks to your fingers, adding more flour if necessary. Dust the dough with flour and leave to rest for 10 minutes.

Put a waffle iron (12 cm/4½ inches in diameter) into the embers for a few minutes; it should be hot but not glowing.

Divide the dough into about 16 walnut-sized balls. Take the waffle iron out of the fire, grease it with oil, place a dough ball in it and close it firmly. Put the iron into the embers and bake the waffle for about 1–2 minutes. Take the waffle out of the iron with a wooden stick. Allow it to cool on a wooden board, tree bark or a lid. After every two waffles grease the waffle iron again.

Variation
You can vary the spices for the waffles as you wish. Spices you might use include: cardamom, orange zest and saffron powder.

Tips
The delicious crispy waffles taste very good plain; or you can put some nut spread on them. They can be accompanied by campfire coffee or chai, an Indian spiced milky tea.

Cooking utensils
Cast-iron waffle iron (or communion wafer iron) with a diameter of about 12 cm/4½ inches and long handles; pastry brushes made of grasses; a bowl for the dough; a whisk (perhaps made out of a ramified branch).

Fire
A mature fire with a lot of embers.

WILDERNESS CRUNCH
Too tempting

This is irresistible for young and old alike.

250 g (½ lb) 2 cups nuts, e.g. hazelnuts, walnuts, almonds and beechnuts

In a pan, dry roast the nuts for a few minutes, stirring constantly. Place the nuts in a kitchen towel and crush loosely with a stone.

200–250 g (7–9 oz) ½–¾ cup acacia honey, according to sweetness desired

Slowly heat the honey in a pan or pot, stirring constantly. When it starts bubbling and foaming, add the nuts. Simmer and stir until the honey is golden brown and smells of caramel.

Pour the mixture on to a flat stone, large leaf or greaseproof paper and spread out to about 2–3 cm (¾–1¼ inches) thick. Allow it to cool and then break it into pieces.

Tip
Caution, especially when preparing this dish with children: when caramelizing honey, it may spit.

Cooking utensils
A pot or pan; a wooden spoon or stick; a cooking pot lid; a flat stone; a large leaf such as burdock or butterbur, or greaseproof paper.

Fire
Fire with not too high flames.

Variation: butter crunchy

about 3 tbsp butter

250 g (9 oz) 3/4 cup sugar or honey

125 g (8 oz) 1 cup nuts

Melt butter and sugar in a pan for 10 minutes, stirring constantly, until the mixture caramelizes. Stir in the dry-roasted nuts and pour the mixture on to a flat surface as above.

LITTLE RED RIDING HOOD'S BUNDT CAKE
Straight out of a fairytale

It never ceases to amaze me how you can bake such delicious cakes over an open fire. Try this method with your favourite cake recipe.

For 1 large bundt cake tin

6 eggs

150 g (5¼ oz) ¾ cup sugar

200 g (7 oz) 1 cup quark

4 tbsp raisins

zest of 1 lemon

250 g (8 oz) 2 cups flour

1 tsp baking powder

140 g (5 oz) ½ cup butter

1 pinch salt

Separate the eggs and mix the yolks with the sugar in a bowl until creamy. Stir in the quark, raisins and lemon zest. Mix the flour and baking powder and add to the bowl. Melt the butter close to the fire and mix into the batter. Beat the egg whites with the salt and fold in. Fill a buttered bundt cake tin with the batter, but not right to the top.

Cover the bottom of a pot with dry sand and stones to a depth of 4–5 cm/1½–2 inches. Place the cake tin on top. Put the lid on the pot, place the pot in the embers and bake for about 20–40 minutes, depending on the size of the cake (a small bundt cake can be done after 15 minutes). With a thin stick, see if the cake is done: if there is still batter on the stick, the cake is not yet ready.

Take the pot out of the fire. Take the cake tin out and turn out the cake. Let it cool and dust it with icing sugar.

Tip
Little Red Riding Hood's bundt cake is ideal for a children's birthday party at home in the garden. If you want to bake the cake on an excursion, you can bring a ready-made cake mix or prepare the batter at home.

Cooking utensils
A pot with a lid (about 10 cm/4 inches more in diameter than the cake tin); a bundt cake tin; a whisk (perhaps made out of a ramified branch); a lemon zester (or just scrape off the zest with a knife).

Fire
A mature fire with plenty of embers.

CHOCOLATE CAKE IN A DUTCH OVEN
A chocolate dream emerges from the embers

1 packet instant chocolate cake mix for baking when you are on the move (or freshly prepared chocolate cake batter for baking in the garden at home)

According to the instructions on the packet:

eggs, butter and milk

butter or vegetable oil for greasing

Mix the batter in a bowl according to the instructions on the packet.

Grease the inside of a Dutch oven with butter or vegetable oil and put the batter into it. Put on the lid, place the Dutch oven on the embers and shovel some embers on to the lid. After about 5–6 minutes, take the Dutch oven out of the embers and shovel some more embers on to the lid. After about 10–20 minutes the cake will be done. Towards the end of the baking time, perhaps remove the lid and check whether you need more top or bottom heat. To check the cake, insert a thin wooden stick into it; if there is still batter on the stick, the cake is not yet done.

Allow the cake to cool in the Dutch oven and then turn it out on to a board or a plate. Ice the cake with chocolate icing as desired.

Tip
Baking cakes in a Dutch oven requires some experience. However, after two or three attempts you will be able quite confidently to bake any cake that you would bake in a normal oven in a Dutch oven on an open fire.

Variation: chocolate fruit cake
Spread some mascarpone on the cake and cover with wild berries or strawberries (see photograph); or cut the cake in half horizontally and fill it with mascarpone and berries. Instead of mascarpone you could use soy vanilla creamy dessert or ready-made custard.

Cooking utensils
A Dutch oven and a bowl.

Fire
A fire with lots of embers.

CHOCOLATE BANANAS
Sweet delight

See the children's eyes light up in the glow of the fire as they spoon out this delicious dessert.

4–5 ripe bananas (organic if possible)

1 bar of milk chocolate, broken into small pieces

Make a 1–1½ cm/about ½ inch incision in the banana skin, gently part the skin and press 4–5 small pieces of chocolate into each banana. Place the banana, open side up, on the embers. After 10–15 minutes the banana skin will have changed its colour to dark brown and the chocolate will have melted. The dessert inside can now be spooned out.

Variations
Instead of chocolate you can use honey and sesame seeds, or just sprinkle some cinnamon on to the open bananas. For a delicious savoury version, sprinkle curry powder on them, which will taste great with rice dishes.

Fire
A mature fire without flames.

CHOCOLATE LEAVES
Dainty nibbles

200 g (7 oz) 1¼ cups dark cooking chocolate

about 20 g (¾ oz) ¾ cup firm leaves (e.g. hazelnut, ground ivy or oak)

Break the chocolate into small pieces and put it in a pot. Place or hang the pot into a bigger pot full of water and melt the chocolate in this bain-marie, stirring continuously. Do not let any water get into the chocolate.

Pull the leaves through the chocolate, smooth side down, and let them cool, chocolate side up. When the chocolate has hardened, carefully pull off the leaf, which should not be eaten.

Cooking utensils
2 pots.

Fire
A fire with plenty of embers.

SUMMER

Luxuriant summer: season of golden light and the sensuous warmth of the sun on our skin. Season of long days, and nights best spent outdoors. In the open air we can make the natural world our home, and listen to birdsong, murmuring brooks and the gently crackling flames of the open fire. We will see shooting stars as we feast at the campfire and exchange stories.

FISH ON A STICK
Simple and tasty

½–1 fish per person

fresh gutted fish (especially suitable: mackerel, sprat, herring, char)

salt and pepper

lemon juice (optional)

sprigs of herbs of your own choice such as oregano, dill, thyme, sage, tarragon, rosemary, basil, bay leaf, mugwort, marjoram

flour for dusting

Wash the fish thoroughly to remove the layer of slime on the skin; also thoroughly wash the cavity with water and dab dry. Rub the fish with salt and pepper, and drizzle lemon juice over it if desired, inside and out. Fill the fish with the herbs, tied into small bunches so that they will not fall out. Place the fish on a skewer lengthwise from head to tail and dust with flour.

Stick the skewers diagonally into the ground next to the embers – if necessary, secure with a forked branch. First grill in direct heat to make the skin crispy. Then continue grilling at a greater distance from the embers (10–15 cm/4–6 inches), occasionally turning the fish. They will be done after 15–20 minutes.

Cooking utensils
Skewers (finger thick), 1–1½ m/3–5 ft long.

Fire
Fire with lots of embers.

Variation: herring with wild herbs
Fill a gutted and washed herring with wild mustard flowers, wild horseradish (in spring the freshly chopped leaves, from September into winter the finely grated root, alternatively with some rocket leaves) and diced bacon.

Place the herring belly up on a skewer lengthwise from head to tail along the middle bone. Close up the stomach cavity with a small wooden skewer if you wish. Grill slowly over the fire.

GRILLED FISH IN A WICKER GRILL RACK

Make a grill for 1–2 fish out of flexible branches. Soak the grill in water for about 30 minutes before laying the prepared fish on it and fixing them with branches (see photograph). Stick some juniper or herb twigs into the grill as desired.

Hold the grill over the embers, or place across two forked branches, and cook the fish. The amount of time needed will depend on their size; if you have plenty of embers the fish could be done after 10–15 minutes.

The advantage of this method is that you can cook the fish on both sides by turning the grill, and there is no danger of parts of the fish falling off, as with skewers.

FISH IN BREAD DOUGH

Prepare a yeast dough (see Colourful Pizza, page 142) and roll out two oval flat pieces of dough. Season a deboned and skinned fish fillet (salmon or trout) with salt, drizzle with lemon juice and sprinkle wild herbs or dill on top. Lay the fish on one flat piece of dough, place the other piece on top and press together firmly at the edges so that it is well sealed. Let the dough rise for about half an hour and then bake for about 1 hour in a Dutch oven. Cut the fish pastry into slices and perhaps serve with a dip such as mustard and dill or wild herb sauce.

SMOKED FISH
A tangy delicacy

The following fish are ideal for smoking:

trout, mackerel, char, eel, bream, carp, tench, cod

There are various methods of smoking fish outdoors. Here are two:

Smoke chimney

With stones, build a chimney 60–100 cm/2–3 ft high, depending on the size of the fish. Thoroughly insulate any spaces between the stones with damp moss or grass.

In a separate fire, keep producing embers so that you can keep refilling the chimney, using a shovel or a large piece of bark. Cover the bottom of the chimney with embers. On top of this, put beech wood shavings, birch wood shavings, juniper branches and other green branches to produce strong smoke. Beech shavings will give the fish a particularly nice golden colour and a wonderful flavour. The shavings should still be slightly damp so that they produce enough smoke. Depending on their size, the fish will need about 20 hours of constant smoke. This smoking technique is only suitable if you are going to be in the same place for at least 1–2 days and the smoke does not bother anyone.

Preparing the fish for smoking

Gut the fish and wash them thoroughly inside and out. You do not have to remove the scales, as you do not eat the skin of smoked fish. Pickle the fish by immersing them in brine (60 g (2 oz) ¼ cup of salt per litre (2 pints) 4 cups of water), covering them and putting in a cool place for about 8 hours. Then take the fish out, dab them dry and hang them in the chimney to smoke. We fashioned some string out of nettle stems, but you can also use wire or string to hang the fish on the crossbars.

This smoking method is still used, on a larger scale, by many people living in a traditional way such as the North American Indians to conserve fish (e.g. salmon).

SMOKE TIN

To make this smoke box in the form of a tin you will need the following:

1 tin can – about 10 litres (21 pints) 42¼ cups (e.g. from a restaurant or snack bar)
400–500 g (14–18 oz) 3–4 cups smoking sawdust (made of fine sawdust, e.g. beech wood or birch wood and aromatic plants such as juniper branches and berries, thyme sprigs, sage leaves and bay leaves, fresh or dried)
about 2 m/6½ ft of strong wire
about 2 m/6½ ft of thin wire, not coated with plastic, or string
1 roll of aluminium foil

2–4 fish, depending on their size, washed, gutted and salted, or fish fillets with skin (e.g. salmon or trout)

Cover the bottom of the tin with smoking sawdust about 2–3 cm/¾–1¼ inches deep. Make holes on either side of the tin at about 4–5 cm/1½–2 inches from the top. Feed the strong wire through one hole and fix it on the outside with a small twig. Salt the fish, string the fish on to the wire (by the gills), feed the wire through the opposite hole and fix it with a small twig there as well. If the fish are too long, their tails can be bent over. Do not hang the fish too close together, so that they are smoked well from all sides.

Place aluminium foil over the top of the tin and fix it with the thin wire like a lid. Pierce some holes in the foil so that the smoke can escape (if you have the lid of the tin, stab some holes into that and use it to close the tin: see page 104).

Place the mini smoking oven into the embers or on a grill above the embers. The bottom of the tin will heat up and the smoke from the smouldering sawdust will rise and give the fish a special flavour. Depending on the size of the fish, this will take around 20–40 minutes. By then the fish will have acquired a golden-brown colour and a spicy smoky aroma.

Fire

A fire with a good layer of embers for a maximum of 30 minutes of even smoking, or perhaps a keyhole fireplace so that you can constantly produce new embers.

SALMON ON A BOARD JAPANESE STYLE
A festive delight

This recipe comes from Kalani Souza, a Hawaiian healer, shaman and environmental activist. If you are lucky enough to be numbered among his friends, you will always enjoy his wisdom as well as his exotic cuisine.

Serves 4

1 side of salmon or
1 salmon fillet without
skin, 700–800g
(1½ –1¾ lb), organically
farmed or wild

2 tsp gomasio (sesame
salt, from a health
food shop)

Marinade:

2 garlic cloves,
finely chopped

2 tsp fresh ginger,
finely chopped

4 tsp sugar

175 ml (6 fl oz)
¾ cup soy sauce

Make a paste out of all the ingredients for the marinade. Rub this into the fish and leave the fish to rest in a cool place for about 1 hour, wrapped in aluminium foil. Sprinkle the sesame salt on both sides of the fish, fix the fish to the board and cook it in an ember pit (see page 88).

Tips
Take the rest of the marinade or newly made marinade and reduce until it caramelizes. Add some more sugar and soy sauce if you wish. Serve with the salmon.

Salmon is ideal for grilling. It has firm meat and lots of flavour of its own. Because it has a tough skin it can easily be fixed on a board without any of the flesh dropping into the embers. It also has very few thick bones, which are easy to remove.

Wild plant information
Japanese salmon goes very well with 'wilderness sushi'. Instead of seaweed simply boil coltsfoot leaves in salted water until soft, chill and cut into rectangles. Then spread on these layers of rice and a paste of finely chopped herbs (such as garlic mustard, wild garlic leaves, watercress or wild mustard leaves, individually or mixed) and roll them up firmly. You can also add some grated horseradish or wasabi powder to the filling. Season with salt.

SALMON ON A SNOWSHOE GRILL
A touch of adventure

How do you best grill a very large piece of skinless salmon on both sides? We let ourselves be inspired by an adventure story about a snowshoe grill from the far north, in which Hannes and Berko built one to their own design.

Serves 6–8

1 side of salmon, skinned,
1–1½ kg (2¼–3⅓ lb),
organically farmed or wild

sea salt

Take a tree trunk 2–3 m/6½–10 ft long and about 5 cm/2 inches in diameter (hazel, birch, alder or ash) and carefully split it down the middle. Tightly wrap the trunk at both ends with string or wire so that the split does not open any further. Put a wedge in the middle to make an oval split, which should be a few centimetres longer than the fish. Add some wicker or hazel cross bars and perhaps fix with nails. The grill now resembles a snowshoe. Soak the snowshoe grill in water before using it.

Season the fish with salt, lay it on the snowshoe grill and use young green bark from the branches you used above to tie the salmon to the grill. Stick two forked branches into the ground on either side of the fire. Place the snowshoe grill on top of them, about 20–60 cm/ 8–23 inches above the embers, depending on the size of the fire and the bed of embers. Cooking time will be 1–2 hours, depending on the size of the fish; turn it occasionally. Through slow grilling the fish will stay juicy and aromatic.
Serve with potatoes and toasted bread.

Cooking utensils
A snowshoe grill (see above); 2 forked branches.

Fire
A large ember fire where you can make new embers in one corner. The fish should be grilled only above embers and not above flames.

SALMON ON A BOARD
A delicious speciality from the far north

Salmon and sea salt: that's all you need for this delicious salmon dish from Scandinavia. This traditional dish originated with the Sami, the indigenous people of northern Scandinavia.

I discovered this recipe on a wilderness trip in northern Finland, where we prepared fish on a campfire on a lake shore, surrounded by endless woods. Lying in our sleeping bags we heard the melancholy howl of wolves. Under the starry sky and with the comforting smell of embers, we fell into a contented sleep.

Serves 6–8

1 very fresh side of salmon, with skin, 1–1½ kg (2¼–3⅓ lb), organically farmed or wild

sea salt

Bore some holes (6–8) into a wooden board and soak it in water for about 2 hours.

Rub the salmon with sea salt, lay it on the board skinside down and fix it with wooden pegs in the pre-bored holes. Place the board on the edge of an ember pit with the fish side towards the embers.

After 10 minutes, turn the board so that the fish is cooked evenly. The fish will be done after about 20 minutes. Gently prod the fish with your finger: it should be soft and flaky. Serve on the board.

Tip

For small sides of salmon you can also use a tree disc, turning it several times during the cooking process.

Cooking utensils

An untreated wooden board, slightly longer and wider than the salmon – hardwood is particularly suitable (an additional aroma can be achieved with beech wood, cedar wood or cherry wood); 6–8 wooden pegs carved out of branches with a knife or an axe and sharpened on one side; drills or tools with which to bore the holes.

Fire

An ember pit: keep a fire burning for about 2 hours in an earth pit 30–40 cm/12–16 inches deep, 1 m/3 ft long and 50 cm/1½ ft wide until there is a bed of embers 10 cm/4 inches deep. Or you can prop up the salmon from the back with a wooden stick next to a normal fire with a lot of embers. However, the fish will turn out more tender and evenly cooked in an ember pit.

Wild plant information

This dish is best served with potatoes baked in the embers, and cucumber or wild herb salad made with common hogweed stems. Peel the stems, cut them into pieces and blanch in a little boiling water. Allow to cool and marinate in olive oil, lemon juice and sea salt. Use only young stems and sprouts of hogweed gathered before they bloom.

According to a Russian recipe hogweed stems can also be fried. Boil them in salt water, season with salt and pepper, sprinkle with breadcrumbs and deep-fry.

ONION VARIATIONS
Wholesome and tasty

With their layers of outer skin, onions are naturally well protected. Therefore they last for a long time and are ideal for the wild kitchen on the move. They can be prepared in many ways. If, for instance, you cook them slowly in hot ashes, the strong onion taste develops an unexpected sweetness and absorbs the smoky scent of the fire; this shows the onion in a completely new light. For the following recipes Spanish onions are best. Use similar-sized onions so that cooking times are the same.

ONIONS IN THE EMBERS

Use onions with as many skin layers as possible; these replace the aluminium foil which is usually used to cook vegetables in the embers.

To make an ember pit, dig about 5 cm/2 inches into the ground. Take some embers out of a fire and lay them in the pit. Place the onions into this pit and cover with hot ashes. Turn the onions several times during cooking. Depending on the size of the onions, cooking time will be around 30 minutes. The skin will become blackened and the inside soft. Now simply cut the onions in half, sprinkle with sea salt, drizzle with olive oil and enjoy.

I sprinkle the ember onions with my own spice mix of ½ tsp of coarse sea salt, 2 threads of saffron, 2 black peppercorns, 1 clove and 1 pinch nutmeg, pestled together in a mortar. This is enough for 4–6 onions.

ONIONS WRAPPED IN CLAY

Wrap whole unpeeled onions with herbs such as thyme, rosemary and marjoram, thinly coat with clay or dough (see pages 56–9) and cook on a bed of embers.

ONIONS IN A DUTCH OVEN

Halve large unpeeled onions lengthwise. Put some oil in a Dutch oven and place the onions on the bottom, cut side up. Baste them with a marinade of olive oil, balsamic vinegar, salt, pepper and chopped herbs such as sage, oregano, thyme and rosemary. Put the Dutch oven into the embers and cook for 20–30 minutes with little upper heat – i.e. put very few embers on top of the lid.

Stick a clove into each onion. This will give it a unique spicy flavour.

FILLED ONIONS

Peel onions and boil for about 10 minutes in salt water. Take them out of the water, slice a lid off the top and slice off the bottom so that they will stand upright. Slightly hollow them out with a spoon, fill as desired and replace the lid.

Suitable fillings are: boiled rice, diced toast mixed with steamed spinach or wild herbs such as ground elder, nettles, hogweed, cabbage thistle leaves, etc., seasoned with salt and pepper and perhaps nutmeg and marjoram.

Cook the filled onions in a Dutch oven or clay oven for about 10 minutes or for 30–40 minutes on a grill.

POTATO VARIATIONS
Campfire classics

Serves 4

1 kg (2¼ oz) 5½ cups new potatoes

2–3 tbsp oil

1 tsp coarse sea salt

pepper

1 handful garden herbs or wild herbs as desired, chopped

GRILLED POTATOES

Boil the potatoes with their skins on for about 15 minutes in salt water. Halve them, baste the cut surface with oil and sprinkle salt, pepper and chopped herbs over them. Bake until crispy on an oven tray in a clay oven or a Dutch oven, on a hot stone or on a muurikka.

EMBER POTATOES

Put the potatoes with their skins on into the embers, or even better into the hot ashes of a fire. Turn occasionally. When they are done, the potatoes will be black on the outside but soft and flavourful on the inside. Slice open the potatoes lengthwise and serve with sour cream, olive oil, salt or quark with wild herbs. They can be spooned out of the skins. Floury potatoes are the most suitable here.

POTATO SKEWERS

Cut pre-cooked potatoes into quarters and stick them on to skewers. Baste with olive oil, and season with salt, pepper, and paprika or cumin, or mix these with olive oil and baste the potatoes with the mixture. Roast above the embers until golden brown and crispy. The skewers are best served with a dip made with melted Gorgonzola (melted in a small pan above the embers with a little milk or cream).

SWEET POTATOES IN THE EMBERS

Sweet potatoes are ideal for cooking in embers. The delicately sweet aroma of their orange-coloured flesh combines really well with that of the fire. Like other potatoes, they are placed in the hot ashes and occasionally turned. You can also wrap them in aluminium foil or clay.

Ginger butter:

150 g (5¼ oz) ¾ cup butter

2 tsp fresh, finely chopped ginger

1 tsp fresh, finely chopped mint leaves

juice of ½ lemon

salt and pepper

SWEET POTATOES WITH GINGER BUTTER

Peel the sweet potatoes, cut into wedges and cook in a Dutch oven or clay oven. Slightly melt the butter in a pot on the fire. Whisk and add all the other ingredients. Pour the ginger butter on to the hot potatoes.

SWEET POTATOES WITH CAMEMBERT

Slowly cook the sweet potatoes with their skins on in the hot ashes, turning them constantly. Shortly before they are done, take them out, cut them open lengthwise, put some Camembert inside and put them back in the embers for a short time or finish baking in a Dutch oven. Then spoon out the inside of the potato with the Camembert.

SWEET POTATOES IN A DUTCH OVEN

Serves 4

1 kg (2¼ oz) 5½ cups sweet potatoes

6–7 tbsp brown sugar

100 ml (3⅓ fl oz) ½ cup water

2 tbsp butter

Peel the potatoes and slice or cut into wedges. Put in a Dutch oven with the sugar and water. Clear the embers in the centre of the fire and put the Dutch oven in there. Put some embers on the lid of the Dutch oven. Cook the potatoes for 20–30 minutes, stirring occasionally. As soon as the potatoes are soft, keep cooking them without the lid on until all the water has evaporated. Put the butter on them and let it melt. Serve hot. This goes very well with fried or grilled poultry.

BABA GHANOUSH
Aubergine paste from the Bedouins

Serves 4

2 aubergines

2 tbsp sesame paste (tahini, from a health food shop)

1 garlic clove, chopped

2 tbsp olive oil

juice of ½ lemon

salt and pepper

Lay the aubergines next to the embers or on the ashes on the embers, and turn them over repeatedly. As soon as the skin blisters and the aubergines are soft, take them out, let them cool and peel them.

With a fork, mash the flesh in a bowl or on a plate. Mix in the sesame paste, garlic, olive oil and lemon juice. Season with salt and pepper. Arrange on a plate with lettuce leaves and tomato wedges and serve with fresh flatbread.

Cooking utensils
A bowl and a fork.

Fire
A mature fire with embers but without flames.

We spent a week travelling with a group on camels in the Sinai Desert. Our camel train was accompanied by Bedouins wrapped in long robes and wearing blue scarves around their heads. They were responsible for our creature comforts and cooked for us every day on the campfire. At the end of the first day we arrived at a large camp in a mountain valley with a spring. The Bedouins had already prepared the food, this delicious dish of aubergines cooked in the embers. They baked fragrant flatbread on the lid of an old oil barrel. It was a really wonderful meal, requiring very few resources.

Sabine Mader, Ulrike Schmid

MY VEGETABLE TAGINE
A Moroccan-style feast

Serves 4

1 tbsp olive oil

1 onion

3 potatoes

3 carrots

1 courgette

1 red pepper, pitted

1 can chickpeas, rinsed

Sauce:

2 tbsp olive oil

2 garlic cloves, finely chopped

1 tbsp fresh ginger, finely chopped

½ tsp cumin

½ tsp sweet paprika

1 generous pinch turmeric

about 600 g (1⅓ lb) 3¾ cups strained tomatoes

1 bunch flat-leaf parsley, chopped

salt and pepper

Soak the tagine in water for about 30 minutes and dry.

Cut the onions, potatoes, carrots and courgette into thin slices and the pepper into long strips. Grease the bottom of the tagine with oil and cover with onion and potato slices. Layer the carrot and courgette slices on top, lay the pepper strips on top in a star shape and finally put the chickpeas on top of that, pressing everything down a little.

For the sauce, heat the oil in a pan and lightly fry the garlic and the ginger. Add the other spices and continue frying. Add the strained tomatoes and let the sauce simmer for 15 minutes. Add the chopped parsley and season with salt and pepper. Pour the sauce over the vegetables. Put the lid on the tagine and fill the dent in the top of the lid with water. Put the tagine over the embers on a tripod or place on a tagine oven and cook for 1 hour.

Eat straight out of the tagine with flatbread. You can also serve couscous with it (see page 56).

Variation: tagine with goulash
In the tagine, fry 1 kg (2¼ lb) 4½ cups of diced beef or lamb in oil and season with salt and pepper. Then pile the vegetables on top and cook as in the recipe above.

Cooking utensils
A tagine (about 28 cm/11 inches in diameter); a tripod or a tagine oven; a small pot for the sauce.

Fire
A keyhole fireplace or a fire with enough embers, or wood charcoal for a tagine oven.

Tips
Vegetarian dishes, meat, fish and poultry alike can be prepared gently and deliciously in a tagine. Serve with Moroccan tea in glasses. This is easily prepared as follows: mix equal parts of green tea and Moroccan mint (fresh leaves are best, but dried will do), pour boiling water over it and leave to steep for a few minutes. Sweeten to taste with sugar. In Morocco this tea is served very sweet.

MEAT AND VEGETABLES IN AN EARTH OVEN
Snug as a bug in a rug

The wilderness teacher and ranger Hannes Kostron says: 'The cooking pit is an efficient cooking method when you're out of doors in winter. You light a fire in the pit and cook your supper on it. While you're enjoying your meal, you heat the stones, and before you go to sleep you can put a whole chicken in the pit to cook. Then you lie in your sleeping bag directly on this "underfloor heating", and you'll be warm and snug all night long. The next day you simply dig up your lunch.'

pieces of meat, depending on the size of the leaves

olive oil

salt and pepper

fresh or dry herbs

large leaves of burdock, butterbur, coltsfoot or cabbage

pepper, courgette, aubergines, pumpkins, potatoes or other vegetables, unpeeled, whole or halved depending on the size of the leaves

Rub the pieces of meat with a marinade of oil, salt, pepper and herbs and individually wrap them in the leaves. Wrap the vegetables in leaves, together with the herbs, in the same way. Fix with small wooden skewers or fold into a package (see page 122).

Dig a 60–80-cm/2–2½-ft deep earth pit in dry soil. Lay the turf you remove aside so that you can replace it after cooking. Lay stones in the pit. Make a fire on the stones and let it burn for 2 hours. Take out any excess large pieces of wood; you can use them for a new fire. Put a layer of grass at least 10cm/4 inch thick on the stones. Lay the vegetable and meat packages on this, put another slightly thinner layer of grass or leaves on top and then fill up the pit with hot stones (from the sides) and earth.

The cooking pit must be filled quickly so that the stones do not cool down too much and the grass does not burn. You can make a new fire on top of the pit to speed up the cooking process. It should burn for about 1 hour. Depending on its size, the food in the pit should be cooked after about 3 hours; without the fire on top of the earth pit cooking time increases by 1 hour. Fish, depending on the size, takes only about 1 hour. Carefully open the pit and remove each layer individually. Refill the cooled earth pit and replace the grass surface.

Cooking utensils
1 shovel and/or a spade.

Fire
Earth-pit fire.

MOMOS
Vegetarian dumplings on a wicker mesh

I discovered momos during my first trip to Dharamsala. This place at the foot of the Himalayas is the home of the Dalai Lama and new home to many exiled Tibetans. Momos are always a real feast for Tibetans.

Serves 4

Dough:

500 g (1 lb) 3¾ cups flour

½ tsp salt

about 1 cup water

Filling:

1 onion, finely diced

1 garlic clove, finely chopped

1 tsp finely chopped ginger

2 tbsp vegetable oil

2 cups finely chopped leaf vegetables such as: Chinese cabbage, chard, spinach and 1 bunch flat-leaf parsley, blanched and finely chopped

or wild leaves such as: cabbage thistle, ground-elder, goosefoot, Good King Henry, common hogweed, wild garlic, nettles, chickweed, individually or mixed, blanched and finely chopped

salt, pepper

½ tsp cayenne pepper

about 125 ml (4 fl oz) ½ cup soy sauce

vegetable oil to grease the wicker mesh

For the filling, heat some oil in a pan with the onions and garlic, add the ginger and vegetables or wild leaves and braise for 10 minutes. Season to taste with salt, pepper and cayenne pepper.

In a bowl, knead the flour, salt and water into a firm dough. Add more water if necessary. Roll the dough out to a thickness of about 4 mm on a firm surface with a bottle or a rolling pin. With a glass or beaker cut out circles (7–8 cm/2½–3 inch in diameter) and roll them until they are 1–2 mm thick. Put a heaped teaspoon of the vegetable mixture on each piece of dough, bundle the dumplings up and twist them at the top to seal them firmly (see photographs).

Half fill a pot with water and put three stones in it. Place a wicker mesh on top so that it is above the water level and still 3–5 cm/ 1–2 inches from the rim of the pot. Grease the wicker mesh so that the momos do not stick to it, and place the momos on top. Put the lid on, but do not close entirely, and put the pot on the fire. Steam the dumplings for 10–15 minutes until the dough is translucent. Serve immediately.

Momos, the Tibetans' favourite dish, are dipped in soy sauce or a spicy chilli sauce and eaten with the hands. In Tibet they are also served in a vegetable soup.

Variations
Momos with a mushroom filling
Momos are also delicious with a mushroom filling. Lightly fry finely chopped mushrooms in butter with onions and parsley and season with salt, pepper and herbs. Continue as with the version above.

1 onion, finely diced

1 garlic clove, finely chopped

2 tbsp vegetable oil

1 cup finely chopped Chinese
cabbage or wild vegetables

1 cup finely chopped parsley

1 heaped tsp finely chopped
fresh ginger

400 g (14 oz) 2 cups minced meat

salt, pepper and cayenne pepper

Momos with a meat filling

Lightly fry the onions and garlic in oil. Add the vegetables, parsley
and ginger. Mix into the minced meat, together with the spices.
Season to taste with salt, pepper and cayenne pepper. Fill the
dumplings with the mixture as described in the previous recipe and
steam.

Cooking utensils

A bowl; a pot; a round wicker mesh, home-made out of fresh wicker
branches, or wedge criss-crossed flexible wicker branches into the
pot (see page 110).

Fire

A small fire with low but powerful flames to keep the water boiling.

'Sit down by a brook
and simply be there.
The song of the water
will take your cares
and bear them
down to the sea.'
Swami Kriyananda

LAMB ON A BED OF HAY
With the scent of the meadow

Serves 4

4–5 tbsp olive oil, plus oil for searing

1 tbsp mustard, ideally Dijon mustard or fig mustard

salt and pepper

4 lamb chops or lamb steaks

about 2 handfuls mountain hay (or dried herbs – see tips)

¼ litre (½ pint) 1 cup vegetable stock

125 ml (4 fl oz) ½ cup white wine

about 125 g (4½ oz) 1 cup flour

Mix the oil with mustard, salt and pepper and rub on the lamb. Leave to marinate for about 2 hours in a cool place (when preparing at home, in the fridge).

Sear the chops or steaks on both sides in hot oil. Put a 2–4-cm ¾–1½-inch layer of hay in a pot, pour on the vegetable stock and white wine and place the lamb on top. Put the lid on. Knead the flour with water into an elastic dough, form a strip as thick as a finger and press it around the outside of the lid so that the pot is sealed. Let it simmer on or close to the embers for about 30 minutes. The meat will absorb the aroma of the herbs and plants, giving it an incomparable flavour.

The lamb is best served with potatoes (see page 92).

Tips

Instead of hay you can use a mixture of dried herbs such as rosemary, thyme, tarragon, hyssop, parsley, marjoram, sage and mint. You can also use wild herbs such as yellow sweet clover, yarrow, sage, red clover, woodruff, thyme, wild marjoram, St John's wort, elderflowers, mugwort and meadowsweet. Gather and dry the herbs one or two days before use.

Following the same recipe you can cook a whole chicken on a bed of hay. Cooking time will be about 1 hour.

Cooking utensils

A pot with a lid or a Dutch oven.

Fire

A fire with embers or low flames.

VEGETABLES ON A BED OF HAY
Inspired by summer

Serves 3–4

about 2 handfuls herb hay made of dried meadow or garden herbs or mountain hay (see page 108)

125 ml (4 fl oz) 1 cup vegetable stock

about 10 small potatoes, ideally new potatoes

2–3 carrots

other vegetables (e.g. Brussels sprouts, courgette, cauliflower etc.)

about 125 g (4½ oz) 1 cup flour

and some water for the dough edge

sea salt

olive oil, horseradish quark or sour cream

Let the herbs dry for 1–2 days. Make a layer of hay at the bottom of a pot, pour the vegetable stock on it and lay the vegetables on the hay, whole or cut into bite-size pieces. Continue as in the previous recipe.

Season the cooked vegetables with sea salt, and then drizzle with olive oil or serve with horseradish quark or sour cream.

This dish goes very well with Feta Cheese in a Coltsfoot Leaf (see page 34) or as an accompaniment to fish or meat.

SMOKED CHEESE
With the savour of fire

a few handfuls smoking sawdust, sawdust or shavings of beech or birch wood

herbs such as lavender, rosemary, thyme, meadowsweet, sage, juniper, fresh or dry

halloumi (Greek cheese for grilling) or pieces of tofu (natural, not smoked)

Cover the bottom of a tin with sawdust and put the herbs on top. Make a grate out of flexible branches about halfway up the inside of the tin: simply cut the branches so that they are slightly longer than the diameter of the tin and wedge them in a criss-cross pattern. Lay the cheese or tofu on the grate. Cover the tin with the lid or aluminium foil, having pierced some holes in it to allow the smoke to escape. Put the tin on the grill above the embers. Soon smoke will come out of the holes in the lid. Depending on the size of the pieces of cheese or tofu, smoke for 10–20 minutes. This will give them a savoury smoky flavour combined with the aroma of the herbs.

Tips

Experiment with this brilliantly simple smoking method by using different types of wood and herbs. The food will always have a unique flavour depending on what you use. You can also add salt. Put some sea salt on a piece of muslin on the wicker grate in the tin and smoke for 10–30 minutes, depending on what intensity of flavour you desire. This is ideal for grilled meat and fish.

Cooking utensils

A tin can (e.g. from a restaurant or snack bar), if possible with a lid, or otherwise aluminium foil to close it; fresh flexible hazelnut or wicker branches; a screwdriver; a nail or something similar with which to stab holes in the lid.

Fire

A small fire with embers, but without flames.

JERKY
Dried meat for rangers

Jerky is meat preserved by a traditional method. When you a have large amount of meat you can easily preserve it this way without a fridge. This method of preserving meat was and is used not only by Native Americans but also in many rural areas worldwide. In North America, jerky is available in most supermarkets and gas station shops. In Europe it is available in petrol station shops and camping equipment stores. It is great snack for when you are on the move and also 'power food' for a strenuous trek, ski tour or snowshoeing trip.

For 125–150 g (4½–5¼ oz) ½–¾ cup of dried meat

500–600 g (1–1¼ lb) 2¼–2¾ cups lean meat (beef, veal, game) – pieces of loin are especially suitable

1 cup finely chopped herbs such as rosemary, thyme or wild herbs such as thyme, meadow sage, marjoram, caraway, mugwort

½ tsp freshly ground pepper

2 tbsp sea salt or rock salt

1 tsp ground spice mixture: allspice, paprika, mace, ginger, fennel seeds, fenugreek, cardamom, juniper berries, cinnamon sticks, coriander seeds, star anise, as desired

Remove any tendons and visible fat from the meat (since fat quickly becomes rancid, jerky containing fat will not keep for so long). Cut the meat into strips 2 to 5 mm (maximum) thick and 5–7 cm/ 2–2½-inches long. In a bowl, mix it well with the herbs and spices, cover and leave to infuse for 1–2 hours.

Hang the meat on a wood structure (see below) so that the individual pieces do not touch each other. The best way is to hang them on twigs or string so that they are exposed to the smoke and dry more quickly. Position the wood structure over the embers of a fire. Put some damp twigs and beech shavings on to the embers to produce more smoke. Wrap a blanket around the wood structure so that the smoke does not escape and penetrates the meat. Important: the meat should not be heated, as if it is the protein will congeal and the meat will not keep. It should not be cooked, only cold smoked. The smoking keeps flies off the meat when you later air-dry it and additionally gives it a savoury aroma.

After about 20 minutes, remove the wood structure and place it in a sunny and airy place. Depending on the amount of sunlight and wind, the meat will be air-dried after 1–2 days; it should be dark brown in colour and have a leathery consistency. If stored in a dry place it will keep for up to a year. The drying process reduces the weight of the meat by about a quarter. You can add the dried meat to soups and stews.

Cooking utensils
A bowl; a wood structure made with branches as thick as a thumb (a tripod with crossbars or a similar structure); a blanket (with no synthetic fibres).

Fire
Fire with embers and without flames (for smoke production).

PEMMICAN
The legendary wilderness food

In many tales from the wild northern forests, pemmican appears as a food supply of the Native Americans, rangers, trappers and gold-seekers. It is their traditional method of preserving meat, since they have neither electricity nor fridges. You could survive on pemmican alone in the wilderness because, unlike pure jerky, it contains fat and the vitamins of the berries. It is one of the highest-energy foods.

4 parts jerky (see page 105), finely chopped

1 part dried berries such as blueberries, lingonberries, barberries, individually or mixed

2 parts pure white bacon fat without meat

Finely grind the jerky with a pestle and mortar or between two stones. Do the same with the berries. Finely chop the bacon and melt it in a pan. Knead everything into a firm dough, divide into small finger-sized pieces and allow them to cool and dry. They will keep for years in sealed plastic bags.

The pemmican can be fried, roasted or baked. Or if you are on the move, cut it into smaller pieces, which can be chewed as a snack.

JUAN-CARLOS PAELLA
A recipe from Valencia

Serves 4–6

3 chicken legs, cut into pieces

olive oil

1 small can pizza tomatoes

1 sprig fresh rosemary,
plus some for garnishing

1–3 garlic cloves

1 generous pinch sweet paprika

1 pinch freshly ground pepper

1/4 tsp cayenne pepper

1 handful green beans, stringed
and cut into 3 cm/1 inch pieces

1 handful thick white beans,
soaked the day before

about 1 1/2 litres (50 3/4 fl oz)
6 1/2 cups vegetable stock

salt

500 g (1 lb) 2 1/2 cups
short-grain paella rice

4 pinches saffron

(saffron threads pestled and
dissolved in warm water)

Brown the chicken pieces in oil in a large pan or a paella pan. Add the tomatoes, rosemary, garlic, paprika, pepper, cayenne pepper as well as the green and white beans, and let it all simmer for about 10 minutes. Now add half of the vegetable stock and season with salt (it should taste a bit too salty, as the saltiness will be reduced when the rice is added).

Add the rice to the pan in a strip down the middle so that chicken mixture is divided in two and some rice is on the surface. Then spread the rice over the paella. Dissolve the saffron in the remaining vegetable stock, gradually add it to the pan and let everything simmer until the rice is done. For an especially delicious flavour leave the paella over the heat so that it is lightly fried.

Cooking utensils

A paella pan or other large pan (inner diameter, about 32 cm/12 1/2 inches) or a muurikka; a small mortar and pestle for the saffron; a stable stand for the pan.

Fire

Small cooking fire with constant flames. Continuously add small branches or logs.

A good friend of mine lived in Spain for a long time and found the love of his life there. He also learnt how to cook the most delicious paella from Juan Carlos of Valencia, who told him that paella used to be cooked on the rice fields surrounding Valencia, on open fires fuelled with rice straw. At that time, the paella consisted of rice, very few vegetables and rat meat – a rather unsavoury story which our children relish.

Sabine Mader

CHICKEN SATAY
Hot stuff – really cool

Serves 4

500 g (1 lb) 2¼ cups
chicken breast fillets

toasted sesame oil for the skewers

Marinade:

2 tbsp fresh ginger, finely chopped

3–4 garlic cloves, finely chopped

2 tsp sugar

2 tsp salt

5 tbsp toasted sesame oil
(from a health food shop)

½ tsp cayenne pepper

15 drops essential lime oil
(from a health food shop)

Dip:

½ cup salted peanut butter

125 ml (4 fl oz) ½ cup coconut
milk (from a can or Tetra pack)

½ tsp cayenne pepper or
1 tsp sambal oelek
(from an Asian food shop)

1 tbsp dark soy sauce

Rinse the meat in cold water and dab it dry. Cut into 1-cm/½-inch long strips and pound them with a piece of wood until they are about ½ cm thick, 2–3 cm/¾–1¼ inches wide and 15–20 cm/ 6–8 inches long (cut lengthwise if necessary). Put them into a bowl. Mix all the ingredients for the marinade well. Cover the chicken strips with the marinade, cover and leave to infuse in a cool place for about 30 minutes.

Meanwhile cream together all the ingredients for the dip.

Grease the skewers with sesame oil and thread the chicken strips on to them. Grill them for 1–4 minutes on each side on a hobo oven with a grill, a hot stone or roof tile or a muurikka until the meat is golden brown and crispy.

Serve with the peanut dip. The chicken can also be served with rice and, as in Thailand, with a spicy cucumber salad or other fresh vegetables.

Cooking utensils
A bowl; 20–25 wooden skewers (15–25 cm/6–10 inches long, depending on the size of the hobo oven); a hobo oven with a grill, a hot stone, a roof tile, a grilling pan, a grill rack or a muurikka.

Fire
A mature fire with lots of embers (the skewers must be grilled above embers, not flames); lots of embers for heating up the hot stone or roof tile. Heat the hobo oven with enough small twigs to achieve a sufficient amount of embers.

GRILLED VEGETABLES
Summer's wealth

vegetables of your choice: fennel, peppers, aubergines, courgettes, onions, sweet potatoes, pumpkin, beetroot, potatoes, asparagus, small artichokes, mushrooms

Marinade:

olive oil

sea salt and pepper

zest of 1 lemon

balsamic vinegar

chopped herbs such as

thyme, rosemary, tarragon or bay leaves

Wash, peel and pit the vegetables as necessary and cut into wedges or slices. Mix all the ingredients for the marinade and spread on the vegetables, or simply season the vegetables with herb salt. Leave to infuse for about 30 minutes.

Cook the vegetables on a hot stone over an ember bed, in a pan, a grill pan, a Dutch oven, a muurikka or a tray in a clay oven, until they are soft inside and crispy outside.

Serve with toasted bread or focaccia and wild herb dips.

Cooking utensils
Any of the following: hot stone, pan, grill pan, Dutch oven, muurikka or clay oven.

Fire
Fire as in the method above.

SUMMER BLOSSOMS IN BATTER
Like snow in summer

Batter:

250 g (½ lb) 2 cups flour

400–500 ml (¾–1 pint) 1½–2 cups milk

3 tbsp sugar or honey

1 pinch cinnamon

2 eggs

1 generous dash beer or 1 tsp baking powder

15 elderflower heads, freshly gathered and cleaned

vegetable oil for deep-frying

Mix all the batter ingredients and leave to rest for 10 minutes.

Dip the elderflower heads in the batter, wipe off any excess on the edge of the bowl and deep-fry the flower heads in oil.

Sprinkle sugar and cinnamon on the fritters as desired. Especially good served with apple purée or wild berry compote.

Variation
Instead of elderflowers you can use the flowers of meadowsweet or acacia.

Cooking utensils
A bowl, a pan or pot.

Fire
Fire with small flames.

HOT FRUIT WITH WILD SYRUP
Simple and succulent

1¼ litres (2 pints) 5 cups water

2 cups finely chopped wild or garden angelica stems and leaves

juice of 1 lemon

2 cups sugar

4–5 large ripe summer fruits such as nectarines, peaches, apricots, pears

Boil the water in a pot, add the angelica leaves and stems, stir and allow to simmer lightly for about 15 minutes; then strain. Add the lemon juice and sugar, and continue boiling until the mixture thickens a bit. Halve the fruit, remove any stones or cores and place the halves cut side up in a Dutch oven. Pour the syrup over them so that it comes halfway up the fruit. Put the lid on the Dutch oven, place it in the embers and cover the lid with embers. If the bed of embers is very deep, push some of the embers aside; place the Dutch oven on a thinner ember bed or on the ground. After about 10 minutes the fruit will be soft and the syrup thick.

Cooking utensils
A pot and a Dutch oven.

Fire
A fire with low flames for the syrup, and a fire with a mature bed of embers for the Dutch oven.

Wild plant information
Wild angelica (Angelica sylvestris) is my favourite medicinal plant. All parts of it have a tangy aromatic scent. It usually grows in damp woods, wet grassland or beside water. It is in the umbellifer family, as is a fatally poisonous plant called poison hemlock. For this reason, gather angelica only when you are absolutely sure you can tell it apart from other plants. Caution: because of its furocoumarin content angelica can cause an allergic skin reaction with sensitive people (see also page 163).

You can also prepare the syrup with other wild herbs. The following plants are suitable: mint, pineapple weed, yellow sweet clover and woodruff (dry a little before use). For a hint of flowers in the flavour use the blossoms of wild rose, violet, elderflower or acacia.

COOKIES IN A LEAF
A crunchy delight

Children love these cookies. Each child can make their own little packet of cookies and bake them.

Makes 12–14 macaroons

2 eggs

2 tbsp sugar or liquid honey

2 cups grated coconut, ground hazelnuts or walnuts

½ tbsp cinnamon for hazelnuts or walnuts

12–14 medium-sized leaves of coltsfoot, lime tree, maple, lady's mantle, all with stems

NUT MACAROONS

Beat the eggs and sugar or honey together until creamy. Mix in the grated coconut or ground nuts, and the cinnamon if you are using nuts, until you have a smooth but not too firm dough.

Put a teaspoon of dough in the middle of each leaf. Fold the sides of the leaves towards the middle; then fold up the stem end and the top end and stick the stem through the top end of the leaf, making a neatly package.

Lay the packages on a hot stone or clay slab and place an upside-down pot, a bowl or the lid of a tagine over them. Caution: the hot stone must not be too hot, as otherwise the packages will burn on the bottom. After 10–15 minutes, depending on the heat and consistency of the dough, the cookies will be ready.

Caution: the pot and the stone will be very hot. Handle them only with fireproof gloves.

Cooking utensils

A bowl for the dough; a whisk (e.g. a home-made one); a hot stone or clay slab; leaves, for baking; a bowl, a pot or a tagine.

Fire

A fire with a sufficient amount of embers for a hot stone or clay slab.

For 10–12 cookies

1 egg

3 tbsp liquid honey

2 tbsp sunflower oil
or melted butter

3 tbsp milk

125 g (4½ oz) 1 cup
wholemeal flour

1 cup oat flakes

1 tsp baking powder

½ tsp cinnamon

1 pinch salt

10–12 medium-sized leaves of
coltsfoot, lime tree, maple, lady's
mantle, all with stems

OAT-FLAKE COOKIES

Whisk the egg with the honey until creamy. Mix in the oil or butter and milk. In a second bowl or in a bag, mix the other ingredients apart from the leaves and then knead into the egg-honey mixture. The dough should not be too firm; if necessary add some milk. Fill the leaves and bake as described on page 122.

Variation

Add raisins, wild berries or chopped chocolate to the dough and place a hazelnut on each cookie.

AUTUMN

Morning mist clothes the trees, their foliage shining gold and bronze in the early rays of the sun. Mushrooms poke their heads through the aromatic forest soil. The bushes are multicoloured, laden with berries. Nature has laid the table; we have only to light our fire. This is truly the 'season of mists and mellow fruitfulness'.

CAMPFIRE COFFEE
A taste of the Wild West

A real cowboy's breakfast – with or without a cowgirl – is not complete without hearty campfire coffee, home-made cowboy beans, and pancakes the way trappers and rangers like them. Sometimes, when a cowboy has a hard day in front of him, a 'power breakfast' is the ideal start. Then he's fit to face cold, wet autumn weather.

ground coffee
(not instant coffee),
2 tsp per cup

Boil water in a jug or pot (the amount depending on how many cups of coffee you are making). Add the coffee. Set aside for a moment, and then boil again on the fire. Take it off the fire. Add a little cold water to make the coffee dregs sink to the bottom. Do not stir.

Tips

Do not fill the jug too full, as the coffee may foam over. Instead of milk you could take milk powder with you. Let the coffee cool down a little before adding the milk powder, as otherwise it could form lumps.

Variation

Add a pinch of cinnamon or cardamom to the coffee shortly before serving, to make spicy Arabic coffee.

Fire

A small young fire with flames that are not too high, or a Swedish log fire.

Cooking utensils

A steel or enamel jug; either a pot or a hobo oven.

Awake expectantly, peel yourself out of your sleeping bag and light a fire. Make coffee in a blue jug and enjoy the scent of the fire and the fir trees. Listen to the morning. Greet the day and take some time.

SOURDOUGH PANCAKES
Gold-seekers' breakfast

Using sourdough as a raising agent gives baking a fresh, slightly sour flavour. It also extends the shelf life of bread and makes it more digestible.

Makes 5–8 pancakes, depending on the size

Sourdough:

500 g (1 lb) 4 cups flour

500 ml (1 pint) 2 cups lukewarm water

to speed up the process: ¼ or at most ½ cube of fresh yeast

Sourdough preparation without yeast

To make a starter dough, mix the flour and water. It should be more liquid rather than too firm, as flour (especially wholemeal flour) thickens in water. Leave to stand at room temperature for 2–3 days and check daily. After a few hours it will already be forming little bubbles; this is a sign that the dough is fermenting. Add a little water or flour as needed, depending on the consistency, so that the dough does not get too liquid or too firm. By checking regularly you can determine whether it is developing lactic acid bacteria and not the undesired acetic acid: the sourdough should smell gently sour and pleasant, not pungent and strong. With the use of wheat flour it can develop a pleasant-smelling apricot aroma, giving the dough a special touch.

Sourdough preparation with yeast

To speed up the fermentation process, add yeast to the dough. This way you can use the sourdough to prepare a yeast sponge. Make a hole in the middle of the flour, add the water, dissolve the yeast in it and then mix the dough.

Using sourdough

Keep the starter (see above) in a container made of glass, clay or porcelain (not metal). Do not seal the container completely, as the fermentation process could burst the container.

Take the required amount of starter dough (for pancakes or bread, two-thirds or three-quarters of the dough) and add flour and water to the rest to make it up to the previous amount. This way you will always have fresh sourdough ready to use. If you do not have time to check the dough daily, just add lots of flour to make it very firm, almost crumbly. You should not use dough that smells strongly of vinegar.

You should take off half of the dough every 7–8 days and refill with flour and water. It is advisable to bake bread or something with the sourdough at least once a week.

For the yeast sponge, mix the sourdough with 1 cup of the flour and the water and let it rise in a warm place overnight. Mix the yeast sponge with the rest of the flour, salt and a little water to make a smooth dough.

To make the pancakes, form round, flat cakes with the dough and bake them in oil in a pan or on a hot stone. Serve with maple syrup to taste.

Baking the pancakes:

1 cup sourdough

400 g (14 oz) 3 cups flour (wholemeal flour is especially good)

250 ml (8½ fl oz) 1 cup water

¼ tsp salt

oil for baking

maple syrup

SOURDOUGH BREAD
The legendary bread of the woodwoses

The trappers, rangers and gold-seekers of northern Canada used to be called sourdoughs. They would spend long periods alone in the wilderness. The starter sourdough was sacred to these quirky woodsmen, because being able to bake bread without yeast meant they would never go hungry. During the hard winters they would keep the dough (which does not tolerate frost) in their beds or close to their warm bodies. A man was awarded the title of Old Sourdough only when he had managed to keep the starter sourdough alive throughout an entire winter in the forest. There are families in Canada and Alaska who proudly claim that the starter sourdough they still use for bread-making was prepared by a distant ancestor – perhaps at the time of the gold rush.

1 cup sourdough

500 g (1 lb) 4 cups flour

2 tbsp sugar

2 tbsp melted butter
(trappers use bear fat)

1 tsp salt

2 tbsp evaporated milk or water,
plus more for getting the dough
to the desired consistency

oil or butter for greasing

Knead all the ingredients into a dough on a floured surface. If the dough is too dry, add some water or milk. Put the dough into a greased pan, cover with a cloth and leave to rise in a warm place for about 1 hour until its volume has doubled.

Form a flat cake out of the dough. Then bake it in the pan, covered with a lid, for about 1 hour.

It is easier to form a loaf out of the dough and bake it in a Dutch oven, a clay oven or like the Large Loaf on page 154. You can also bake this bread in a tagine or a fire pot (earthenware pot with a lid). The bread is done when it sounds hollow when you tap it.

Cooking utensils
Bowl; glass or plastic container for the sourdough; one of the following: pan, hot stone, Dutch oven, fire pot, clay baker or clay oven.

Fire
According to the cooking utensils you use.

COWBOY BEANS
A Wild West classic

Cowboy beans taste great with bacon, eggs, sourdough pancakes and campfire coffee, but also just with toasted bread – for an authentic cowboy atmosphere.

Serves 4

2 cups dried pinto beans or kidney beans

1 cup diced bacon or ham

1 tbsp olive oil

1 onion, chopped

1 cup tomato paste (about 1 tube)

1 tsp mustard

1 tbsp brown sugar

1 tsp sambal oelek
(from an Asian food shop)

pepper and sea salt

Soak the beans in water for 8–10 hours; then strain and bring to a boil in fresh water.

In a pan, heat the oil and fry the diced bacon or ham in it; add the onions and fry until glazed. Add to the beans. Mix in all the other ingredients (apart from the salt) and let everything simmer for at least 1 hour. If necessary, add more liquid. Season with salt at the end.

Cooking utensils
Pot; perhaps a colander for straining; perhaps a pan.

Fire
Fire with low flames and sufficient embers.

CORN-ON-THE-COB VARIATIONS
A seasonal savoury

REALLY EASY CORN COBS

Peel the outer leaves on the corn cob down towards the bottom of the cob, but do not remove them. Remove the fine hairs. Soak the corn cob with the leaves in cold water for about 20 minutes; then shake dry. Fold the leaves back up on to the corn cob and grill on a grill over the embers for 15–20 minutes. Turn several times with grilling tongs (perhaps home-made out of a flexible wicker branch). Then season with salt and spread with herb butter or marinade (see below).

Per corn cob:

1 tbsp olive oil

1 tsp balsamic vinegar

½ clove garlic, finely chopped

1 tsp lemon juice

pepper, paprika, salt

MARINATED CORN COBS

Mix all the ingredients for the marinade.

Cook the corn cobs without leaves in boiling water for about 15 minutes. Take them out and dab them dry. Spread them all over with the marinade and grill on all sides on a grill over the embers for about 10 minutes, turning about three times. Serve with melted butter and season with salt.

CORN COBS IN THE EMBERS

Cover the bed of embers with a layer of ashes and lay the corn cobs on top. Turn several times. Grilling time, depending on size, will be 15–20 minutes.

Tips

Corn cobs with leaves are especially suitable for grilling, as you can grill them gently without having to wrap the cobs in aluminium foil. Corn leaves are suitable for wrapping around feta cheese, vegetables, meat and cookies. Cook them gently on a grill or a hot stone.

You can also serve corn cobs with mint butter made with chopped wild mint, butter and salt.

EGG IN BREAD
Quick and easy

Fancy a fried egg at the campfire? With this recipe it is possible to make one without a pan.

Per person:

1 slice of bread

1 egg

salt, pepper

Heat a flat stone in the embers and lay on it a slice of bread from which you have removed the centre. Break the egg into the hole. As soon as the egg is cooked, take the whole thing off the stone and season with salt and pepper.

Cooking utensils

Flat stone, roof tile or muurikka.

Fire

Lots of embers to heat the stone or roof tile; for a muurikka, a small fire with low flames.

ASH EGGS

An archaic cooking method by which fresh eggs are cooked slowly in the hot ashes. Bury the eggs in the ashes at the edge of the fire. Depending on the heat and maturity of the embers and ashes, you can enjoy your smoke-flavoured breakfast egg after 20–30 minutes. However, this cooking method requires sensitivity. If you heat the eggs too quickly, they will burst. If they do not have enough heat, the cooking process will take much longer. If you bury the eggs in the ashes for several hours or overnight, they will acquire a golden-brown colour and a fine flavour.

POWER BREAKFAST
An old European recipe

3/4 litre (25 fl oz) 3 cups
milk or water

1 pinch salt

125 g (4 oz) 1 cup coarsely
ground spelt flour

1 tbsp butter or clarified butter

Boil the milk with the salt. Gradually add the flour, stirring constantly. Simmer for about 15 minutes, still stirring. If you cook the porridge for long enough, it will acquire a sweetish flavour without the addition of sugar. Take it off the fire and leave it to stand for a moment. When the porridge develops a skin, put the butter on it and let it melt. Serve warm.

This goes well with honey, nuts, raisins or fresh, dried or cooked wild fruit.

Tip
If you are on the move and have no milk you can use powdered milk mixed with water. Clarified butter keeps much longer than butter.

Cooking utensils
Pot, hobo oven or clay pot.

Fire
Fire with small flames.

Our Neolithic ancestors cooked this porridge in clay pots on an open fire; later, metal pots were used. Until recently, porridge was a staple food for many. Spelt, an ancient variety of grain, is particularly suitable for a power breakfast. Over eight hundred years ago the Abbess Hildegard of Bingen praised it thus: 'Spelt is the best of grains. It is rich and nourishing and milder than other grains. It produces a strong body and healthy blood in those who eat it and it makes the spirit of man light and cheerful.'

After a night in the open – especially in autumn, when mornings are often cool – this power breakfast will give you the strength and warmth you need to enjoy an exciting day outdoors.

MUSHROOM STEW
Straight out of a fairy ring

Serves 3–4

500 g (1 lb) 6½ cups mushrooms
(e.g. golden chantarelles, porcini
mushrooms, button mushrooms,
bay boletes)

1 onion, finely diced

2–3 tbsp butter or oil

1 tbsp finely chopped parsley
and/or wild herbs such as
ground ivy, marjoram, thyme

about 1½ cups cream, to taste

salt and pepper

1 pinch ground coriander seeds
(optional)

Sort through the mushrooms, clean them and if necessary cut into pieces.

Glaze the onion in a pan with the butter or oil. Add the mushrooms and herbs and fry lightly. Add the cream and season with salt, pepper, and coriander if you wish.

Serve with Dumplings in a Napkin or Polenta (see pages 150 and 132).

Tips
Do not wash the mushrooms in water, but instead clean them with a pastry brush (e.g. grass bundled together) or a cloth.

Should you wish to have more sauce, simply add some vegetable stock and thicken with flour.

Cooking utensils
Pan.

Fire
Fire with low flames.

Variation: mushroom omelette
Prepare the mushrooms as above, but do not add cream. Whisk 3–4 eggs with 100 ml/½ cup of milk, season with salt and pepper and pour on to the mushrooms in the pan. Leave the omelette for a few minutes until it sets.

'There is more to life than increasing its speed.'

Mahatma Gandhi

POLENTA
To warm the cockles of your heart

Serves 4

salt

1 litre (2 pints) 4 cups water

500 g (17½ oz) 3 cups polenta

pepper and nutmeg

1 tbsp oil or butter

Salt the water and bring to a boil. Gradually pour in the polenta and, stirring constantly, let it simmer lightly for 20–30 minutes. Season with pepper and nutmeg and add butter or oil to taste.

Serve as a side dish with a mushroom stew or game dishes, or make into polenta slices. To make polenta slices, cook polenta in a maximum of ¾ litre (25 fl oz) 3 cups of water. Grease an oven tray, large pan or pot with oil and spread the polenta over it about 2 cm/¾ inch thick. Let it cool and cut it into pieces. Then cook the pieces on a grill, muurikka, hot stone or flat roof tile until golden brown. Or bake them in a closed Dutch oven with upper heat. You can also add cheese slices, pieces of Gorgonzola, mushrooms or wild herbs.

Tip
Polenta also makes a great (sweet) breakfast porridge. Add raisins, nuts and wild berries and give it a finishing touch with milk, cream or yoghurt.

Cooking utensils
A pot. For the polenta slices: a tray or pan and one of the following: Dutch oven, grill, muurikka, hot stone or roof tile.

Fire
Fire with low flames; lots of embers for the Dutch oven

FRIGGA
A hearty meal from the forest

It is said that woodcutters, root-diggers and rangers in Carinthia (Austria) used to prepare this dish on their campfires deep in the forests or high up in the mountains.

Serves 4

oil for frying

200 g smoked bacon, cut into four strips or slices

4 slices, about 5 mm thick, of your favourite hard cheese

4 eggs

salt and pepper

4 polenta slices, pre-cooked, firm, about 2 cm/¾ inch thick (see page 132)

Heat the oil in a pan and lightly fry the bacon. Turn the bacon and cover with the cheese slices. As soon as the cheese begins to melt, crack the eggs on top and leave to set. Season with salt and pepper.

Warm the polenta slices on a stone or a grill rack; then put them on a plate and serve covered with the bacon and egg mixture.

Cooking utensils
Either a pan with a lid or a Dutch oven.

Fire
Fire with embers or a fire with low flames.

PARASOL MUSHROOM SCHNITZEL
My favourite mushroom dish

The parasol mushroom (Macrolepiota procera), Europe's biggest gilled mushroom, grows between July and October in mixed forests, spruce forests and meadows. It is found growing solitarily or in groups and fairy rings. Its imposing plate-sized head has brown scales on a light background and sits on a stalk that can be up to 50 cm/1½ ft long. It has a fine peanutty flavour and is a real feast. It can occasionally be found at vegetable markets.

Important: do not confuse the parasol mushroom with the shaggy parasol (Macrolepiota rhacodes). Gather only mushrooms that you can identify with certainty; when in doubt, consult a local expert. Also take into account the local regulations for the gathering of each mushroom species.

Serves 4

4–5 parasol mushrooms (depending on size)

paprika, salt and pepper

2 eggs

125 g (4 oz) 1 cup breadcrumbs or flour

oil or fat for deep-frying

Remove the stems from the mushrooms. Carefully season the caps with paprika, salt and pepper.

Beat the eggs in a flattish bowl and spread out the breadcrumbs on a flat plate or a large leaf (butterbur, burdock, etc.). Dip the mushroom caps first in the egg and then the breadcrumbs, and deep-fry in hot oil until golden brown.

Variations
You can also dip the mushrooms in beer batter or pancake batter (see page 44 and 178). Porcini mushrooms, orange boletes or button mushrooms are also suitable for deep-frying.

Cooking utensils
A pan or muurikka; 1–2 plates.

Fire
A small fire with low flames.

Wild plant information
Serve the deep-fried mushrooms with wild berry purée (made from lingonberries, blueberries, rowan berries, barberries and/or cornelian cherries).

You can add some ground hazelnuts or walnuts or roasted nettle seeds to the breadcrumbs.

BRUSCHETTA
An Italian snack

A filling snack for when you are on the move or in the garden, bruschetta is said to have been invented by Italian farm workers during the tomato harvest. It is a simple but truly delicious dish – especially good with a glass of red wine to wash it down. With the best ingredients, such as good country bread, the finest olive oil, fresh garlic, sea salt or fleur de sel, freshly ground pepper and fresh sun-ripened tomatoes, bruschetta can measure up to any sophisticated dish. Do not overload the bread; it tastes delicious as it is.

Serves 2

4 slices white bread

2 tbsp finest olive oil

1–2 garlic cloves, halved

1 ripe tomato, halved or cut into wedges

sea salt and black pepper

Roast the slices of bread on a grill, hot stone or skewer on both sides until golden brown.

Spread one side of the warm slices with olive oil and rub with half a garlic clove. Then either rub the bread with a tomato half or lay a tomato wedge on top. Season with salt and pepper.

Tip
Italian country bread is especially suitable for this dish, but you can use any other white country bread, ciabatta or slices of your own Large Loaf (see page 154).

Fire
A mature fire with embers and small flames.

Cooking utensils
A grill, a hot stone or a skewer.

CROSTINI WITH MUSHROOMS
The best of Autumn

Serves 3–4

1 bunch flat-leaf parsley, finely chopped

1 tsp thyme leaves, finely chopped

1–2 garlic cloves, finely chopped

2–3 tbsp olive oil

300 g (10½ oz) 4 cups fresh mushrooms (e.g. porcini mushrooms, golden chantarelles, bay boletes), cleaned, chopped

salt and pepper

1–2 pinch ground coriander seeds

1 loaf white bread, baguette, ciabatta or sourdough pancakes – crusty Italian bread is particularly suitable

Lightly fry the parsley, thyme and garlic in a pan with the olive oil. Add the mushrooms and braise for 10–15 minutes, stirring constantly. Season with salt, pepper and coriander.

Slice the bread and toast the slices on a grill above the embers, on a hot stone or on a skewer. Then spread the mushroom mixture on them and enjoy the bruschettas while still warm.

Tip

Other ingredients that go well on crostini are: herb pâté, liver pâté, olive tapenade, basil pesto, nut pesto, olive oil with freshly chopped herbs such as watercress, dandelion, ground ivy or rocket. If you like the taste of garlic, you can rub the toasted slices of bread with half a garlic clove before spreading the mushrooms on them.

Cooking utensils

A small bowl for mixing, a pan and a grill, a hot stone or a skewer.

Fire

Mature embers without flames for the grill; a fire with lots of embers for the hot stone.

FOCACCIA
The art of Italian baking

Dough:

500 g (1 lb) 3¾ cups flour

1 tsp salt

1 cube fresh yeast or
1 packet dry yeast

250 ml (8½ fl oz) 1 cup
lukewarm water

2 tbsp olive oil

1–2 garlic cloves, finely chopped

1 tbsp olive oil

1 cup finely chopped herbs
(e.g. thyme, oregano, rosemary,
tarragon) or wild herbs (e.g. wild
marjoram, wild thyme, ground ivy)

olive oil for deep-frying

Make a yeast dough with the ingredients (see page 162), mixing 2 tbsp of olive oil instead of sugar into the yeast sponge. Let the dough rise.

Lightly fry the garlic in some olive oil and knead it into the dough, together with the herbs. Form 6–7 balls out of the dough and press them flat. Thoroughly grease the bottom of a pan or Dutch oven with olive oil. Put the flat dough pieces into the pan and cover with aluminium foil or the oven lid. Bake above the embers for about 10–15 minutes. Take off the cover or lid, turn the bread over, re-cover and bake for about another 10 minutes on the other side.

When the focaccia is done, you can drizzle some olive oil on it and perhaps sprinkle chopped rosemary leaves on it.

Cooking utensils

A pan with a lid or aluminium foil to cover, or a Dutch oven.

Fire

A fire with lots of embers.

Variation: fougasse (French olive flatbread)

Add rosemary, thyme and coarsely chopped black olives to the yeast dough. Make 1–2 palm-sized flat shapes out of the dough. Score them with a knife so that the incisions can be seen after baking, like the veins on a leaf. Leave to rise for about 30 minutes. Bake for about 20 minutes in a clay oven. If you use a Dutch oven you will need more heat but a shorter baking time. Spread olive oil on the warm bread to taste.

ROOT CRISPS ON A HOT STONE
Autumn nibbles

parsnip

black salsify

carrot

Jerusalem artichoke

potato

celery root

beetroot

kohlrabi

or: roots of wild plants such as burdock, evening primrose, parsnip

oil

spices such as salt, pepper, chilli, curry

Wash and peel the root vegetables and cut them into very thin slices. Heat a flat stone in the embers, perhaps having greased it slightly with oil, and roast the vegetable slices, occasionally turning them over (see photograph, page 125). Season to taste.

Serve with a variety of dips – spicy or with herbs, with or without garlic – or garlic butter.

Tips
These crisps make a great snack for when you are on the move. You can easily take some root vegetables with you or gather them outdoors, and flat stones can be found virtually anywhere.
You can also make root crisps on a muurikka.

Wild plant information
Burdock is found on riverbanks and at the edges of paths. Its large root is particularly suitable for this dish. You can harvest it in autumn and winter. The roots of a one-year-old plant are best, as in the second year it becomes woody. To harvest burdock roots you need a spade or shovel, since the plant has a very deep taproot. Burdock roots taste similar to those of black salsify.

Cooking utensils
A hot stone, a roof tile or a muurikka.

Fire
A fire with lots of embers to heat the stone or roof tile; a small fire for the muurikka.

ACORN FLATBREAD WITH WILD BERRY PURÉE
Tasty survival food from the Stone Age

A Native American in North America taught me how to make acorn flatbread. She put the peeled acorns in a basket and hung it in a small waterfall to rinse out the tannins. Since European acorns often have a higher tannin content than American ones, they should be boiled several times.

For 8 flatbreads

1 kg (2¼ lb) 8¼ cups acorns
(remove any worm-eaten ones)

salt or honey

Peel the acorns, coarsely chop them and slightly grind them between two stones. Boil in a pot of water for about 10 minutes, strain and boil again in fresh water. Depending on the tannin content of the acorns, repeat the boiling process several times until the water is clear after boiling.

Strain the acorns and leave them to dry in the sun or dry them in a large pan on the fire, and then lightly roast them. Then grind them to a smooth consistency between two stones. Season the mixture with salt or add honey, knead thoroughly, form small balls and press flat. If the dough is not sticky enough, add some water or flour to the mixture; you can also add milk, yoghurt or quark. Bake on a hot stone, roof tile or muurikka.

Tips
Do not pick acorns from a tree; just pick up the ripe ones from the ground.

Acorns are easier to peel if you lightly roast them on the fire: they will burst open.

You can also add raisins, wild berries, bread seasoning and/or nuts to the dough.

Cooking utensils
A pot for boiling the acorns; stones for grinding; a hot stone, roof tile or a muurikka.

Fire
A fire with low flames for cooking; a fire with a lot of embers for heating the flat stone or roof tile; a fire with low flames for the muurikka.

Wild plant information

You can serve the acorn flatbread with wild berry purée. Just boil elderberries and stoned cornelian cherries to a purée and sweeten with honey.

COLOURFUL PIZZA
A vegetarian feast

Alexandra Como prepared this pizza for us in a clay oven. It was delicious!

For 1 large tray of pizza
or 4 small round pizzas

Dough:

1 cube fresh yeast

½ tsp sugar or honey

150 ml (5 fl oz) ¾ cup lukewarm water

400 g (14 oz) 3 cups wheat or spelt flour

1 tsp salt

1 generous dash olive oil

Toppings:

1 aubergine, cut into thin strips

1 courgette, sliced

2 garlic cloves, sliced

olive oil for frying

150 ml (5 fl oz) ¾ cup strained tomatoes or tomato sauce from a barrel (see page 145)

oregano and salt

1 quantity of pizza dough (see page 49)

2 tbsp olive oil

1 tsp sea salt

1 handful fresh dandelion leaves (or rocket leaves)

50 g (1¾ oz) ¼ cup fresh Parmesan (whole)

coarsely ground pepper

To make the dough, mix the yeast and sugar or honey with the lukewarm water and leave to rest for 5 minutes. Add the flour, salt and olive oil and knead into an elastic dough. If the dough is too dry, add some water. Leave the dough to rise in a warm place for about 30 minutes. Then knead it again, roll it out and lay it on a greased oven tray. Alternatively, divide the dough into 4 and make round pizzas which can be baked individually in a Dutch oven.

While the dough is rising, fry the vegetables (apart from the tomatoes) in a pan with oil. Spread the tomatoes on the rolled-out dough, lay the other vegetables on them and sprinkle salt and oregano on top. Bake the pizza in a clay oven (pre-heated for about 1 hour) for 5–10 minutes. In a Dutch oven with embers on the lid, the pizza will take 5–8 minutes.

Cooking utensils
A clay oven or Dutch oven; an oven tray for the clay oven; a bowl for the dough; a pan.

Fire
A well pre-heated (about 1 hour) clay oven; or for a Dutch oven, a fire with plenty of embers.

PIZZA WITH DANDELIONS: WILD LEAVES ON A CRISPY DOUGH
Prepare the dough as above. Before baking, brush it with olive oil and sprinkle sea salt on top. Bake on an oven tray in a clay oven or directly in a Dutch oven as above; the pizza should be crispy and not too soft. Put the dandelion leaves on the baked pizzas, sprinkle coarse Parmesan shavings on top and season with pepper to taste. You could also perhaps drizzle on some high-quality olive oil.

TOMATO SAUCE FROM A BARREL
Preserving in large quantities

With this method you can keep a year's supply of aromatic tomatoes in jars for delicious soups, pizzas, sauces, etc. I learned this recipe in Tuscany, where we prepared it in late summer in the garden in front of our house. Of course you should not cook such a quantity of tomato sauce alone; use it as an opportunity to be together, chatting, or just gazing into the fire . . . Buon divertimento!

Makes about 18 litres
(38 pints) of sauce

20 kg (44 lb) ripe, aromatic
tomatoes (San Marzano
tomatoes are best)

2 bunches fresh basil

Pour boiling water over the tomatoes or briefly blanch in a pot with boiling water. Take them out, skin them, halve them and take out the pulp (not necessary with very ripe tomatoes). Finely dice the tomatoes or, depending on what you want to use them for later, halve them or cut into wedges. Put the tomatoes into clean glass jars with 1–3 basil leaves (whole or torn) in each jar and close firmly. Wrap each jar in newspaper (this prevents the jars from cracking).

Place a barrel in the fireplace. Put the jars in the barrel and fill with water until the jars are covered. Light the fire under the barrel. As soon as the water starts boiling, leave for about another 40 minutes. Leave to cool for few hours and take the jars out of the barrel. In the sealed jars the tomato sauce will keep for at least 1 year.

Tip
Do not salt the tomatoes, or else they will release water and the sauce will be too watery. Season the sauce when you use it.

Cooking utensils
A large pot for hot water for skinning the tomatoes; a metal barrel (uncoated and unpainted); different-size glass jars with screw tops; newspaper.

Fire
Fireplace with stones or a strong grill to hold the barrel and support it over a not-too-high fire for a longer period of time.

VENISON STEW
Peasant-style game

We made the venison stew in true rustic style in a clay pot we fired ourselves.

Serves 4–6

3 onions, finely chopped

3 garlic cloves, finely chopped

oil for frying

1 kg (2¼ lb) 4½ cups venison (neck, shoulder or haunch), fat and tendons removed, diced

6 coriander seeds

1 bay leaf

6 juniper berries

3 cloves

6 peppercorns

1 sprig of thyme (or 1 tsp dried thyme)

salt and pepper

⅛ litre (4¼ fl oz) ½ cup red wine

½ l (1 pint) 2 cups venison stock (or vegetable stock)

1–3 tbsp flour

⅛ litre (4¼ fl oz) ½ cup cream

Lightly fry the onions and garlic in oil. Add the diced meat, brown, add the herbs spices and deglaze with the red wine and stock. Let it simmer on a medium heat for about 1 hour (depending on the pot you use and the fire). If necessary, add more liquid. As soon as the meat is soft and tender, take it out of the sauce, strain the sauce through a sieve and put both back into the pot. Mix the flour and cream, add them to the sauce and leave the sauce to simmer until it has thickened.

Serve with Dumplings in a Napkin (see page 150), potatoes, noodles or polenta, and – especially tasty – Barberry Compote (see page 160).

Tips

Dry roast the spices, apart from the bay leaf and salt, in a pan for 1–2 minutes before use and grind between two stones or with a pestle and mortar. This intensifies the aroma.

You can give the sauce a finishing touch by adding about 2 tbsp of lingonberry (cowberry) compote. If you add the zest of ½ lemon to the spices, this will give the sauce a tangy flavour.

Cooking utensils

A pot, casserole or clay pot (see photograph); a sieve.

Fire

For the pot or the casserole a fire with low flames; for the clay pot a bed of sufficient embers

VENISON IN AN EARTH PIT
Primitive yet sophisticated

venison, cut into pieces
herbs and wild spices (e.g. thyme,
meadow sage, wild marjoram,
juniper berries, mugwort, caraway)

large leaves (cabbage,
burdock, butterbur)
raffia or string

Lightly season the meat with salt and pepper and wrap it in wild herb sprigs or rub with finely chopped wild herbs. Wrap the meat in the leaves and tie it up with raffia or string. Dig an earth pit about 50 cm/1½ ft deep, the size depending on the amount of meat. Line the pit with stones. Light a fire in the pit and let it burn for about 2 hours. When the fire has burned down, cover the bed of embers with a layer of fresh grass and lay the prepared meat packages on top. Cover them with another layer of grass and then fill up the pit with earth and hot stones. Light a fire on top and let it burn for 1–1½ hours. Open the earth pit after 2–3 hours – the length of time needed will depend on the size of the pieces of meat – and take out the cooked meat.

Tip
The slow cooking process leaves game especially tender and juicy.

VENISON IN A POT IN AN EARTH PIT
Earthy cuisine

1 venison roast (rolled roast)

oil or clarified butter for frying

root vegetables (e.g. potatoes, carrots, parsley root, onions), coarsely chopped

peeled chestnuts (optional)

various herbs and wild spices such as thyme and rosemary twigs, bay leaves, juniper berries, plus additional finely chopped herbs

vegetable stock

salt, pepper, and perhaps allspice and nutmeg

about 100 g (3½ oz) ¾ cup flour and some water for the dough rim

Sear the venison on all sides in oil or clarified butter in a Dutch oven or a roaster with a lid. Take it out.

Cover the bottom of the Dutch oven or roaster with root vegetables and, if you wish, chestnuts. Add the herbs and wild spices. Pour in enough vegetable stock to cover the vegetables. Mix the chopped herbs with salt, pepper, allspice and nutmeg to taste and some oil, rub them into the meat and place the meat on top of the vegetables.

Put the lid on and, if necessary seal with a roll of dough (see page 102).

Dig an earth pit about 2–3 times deeper than the height of the pot, leaving about 10 cm/4 inches between the pot and the ground for the bed of embers. Now make a fire in the pit; start with a lot of thin twigs or thin logs and later add hardwood logs (e.g. beech or oak). After about 2 hours, let the fire burn down. Remove about three-quarters of the embers, put the Dutch oven or roaster on the bed of embers and put the rest of the embers on top and around the sides. Cover everything with the earth you dug out of the pit and let the roast cook, depending on the size, for about 2–3 hours. Open the pit and take out the pot.

Tip

You can prepare any kind of roast in this way. With time you will acquire enough experience to know exactly how long the meat needs to cook in the earth pit so that it is tender and juicy.

Variation

This cooking method is especially good for poultry. We once prepared a guinea fowl for a New Year's Eve meal in this way. Simply sear the guinea fowl, season it, wrap it in bacon and cook it on vegetables such as carrots, onions and chestnuts in a roaster as above.

Cooking utensils

A Dutch oven or roaster; a shovel and/or spade.

Fire

Fire in an earth pit.

DUMPLINGS IN A NAPKIN
From Grandma's recipe book

On a canoe trip in the Swedish woods we found plenty of golden chantarelles, so we made a lovely mushroom stew out of them and prepared these dumplings in a napkin to go with it. They turned out perfectly.

Serves 3–4 as a side dish

250 g (9 oz) 1½ cups old bread rolls or white bread, diced

5 tbsp flour

1 onion, finely chopped

2 tbsp oil or butter

1 cup finely chopped parsley or wild herbs

1 tsp salt for the dumplings

¼ litre (8½ fl oz) 1 cup milk

2 eggs

1 tbsp flour for dusting

salt for the water

Mix the diced bread and the flour in a bowl. Lightly fry the onion in the oil or butter, add the herbs and salt, continue frying for a bit and then add to the bread. Whisk together the milk and eggs, pour them over the bread and mix everything well. Leave to rest for 30 minutes and then knead thoroughly.

Roll the dough on a floury surface into a thick roll. Lay this on a napkin, wrap it up and tie at both ends with string. Let the roll simmer in plenty of salty water for about 30 minutes.

Take it out, remove the napkin (having first rinsed with cold water to make it easier to remove the napkin) and cut the dumpling into finger-thick slices. This goes very well with game or mushroom dishes.

Variations
Add roasted bacon bits, braised finely chopped mushrooms or fresh, finely chopped wild garlic to the dough.

Cooking utensils
A bowl; a small pan or pot to fry the onions in; a large pot to boil the dumpling in; a napkin; some string.

Fire
A fire with small flames to boil the water, or a hobo oven heated with small branches.

FERN DIP
Scent of the wild

I love the polypody fern and it never ceases to surprise me how delicious its roots are. I wanted to immortalize it in this book with a very special recipe. So I asked Markus Stöckle, a young and ambitious chef and lover of molecular cuisine, to help me develop a polypody dip – and here it is.

3–4 fresh polypody roots
(makes 2 tbsp finely chopped)

2 tbsp finely chopped fresh ginger

1 small onion, finely chopped

1 garlic clove, finely chopped

50 g (1¾ oz) ¼ cup butter

200 ml (6¾ fl oz) ¾ cup
white wine for deglazing

1 tsp salt

1 pinch pepper

1 tsp sugar

1 litre (2 pints) 4 cups water

1 tbsp flour

1 tbsp flat-leaf parsley,
finely chopped

Wash the polypody roots, remove the small side roots, peel with a knife and finely chop. Lightly fry in a pan with the ginger, onion and garlic in 20 g (¾ oz) 1¼ tbsp of the butter. Deglaze with a third of the white wine and let it boil down. Repeat the deglazing two more times with the rest of the wine, leaving it to boil down each time. Season with the salt and pepper, add the sugar and pour on the water.

Mix the flour with the remaining butter, crumble into the sauce and stir in well. Let the sauce simmer without a lid for about 2 hours until it is creamy. Strain and add the finely chopped parsley.

Tip
You can serve this sauce with its indescribable, wild aroma as a dip with game dishes and braised meat. You can also use it to glaze a game roast.

BEAR SUGAR
Caramelize finely diced polypody root and ginger: heat 3 tbsp of sugar in a pan and let it caramelize, stirring vigorously. Add finely diced polypody root and ginger, stir and spread out on a board. When it has cooled down, crumble and sprinkle over game dishes.

Wild plant information
Polypody (Polypodium vulgare) has sweet-tasting roots. The fern, about 20 cm/8 inches high, has little brown dots on the lower side of the fronds. It mainly grows in deciduous and mixed forests and can be found on mossy rocks and sometimes in the tree forks of old trees and in cracks in stone walls. Its roots possess great healing powers: it benefits the liver and gall, aids digestion and is also a natural anabolic agent (muscle-building agent).

CHESTNUT VARIATIONS
The essence of autumn

How about a convivial evening round the fire with chestnuts? Chestnuts can be prepared in many ways. Their scent is part of autumn and winter. Naturally well packed, they are easy to carry and prepare on the move. They cook quickly and you can either bring the flatbread to go with them or bake it in the embers. Red wine will add to the warm glow . . .

CHESTNUTS IN THE EMBERS
Cut an X into each chestnut shell with a sharp knife on the bulging side and lay the chestnuts in a 1:1 mixture of embers and ashes. Move the chestnuts around occasionally during the cooking process. After about 10 minutes they will be ready to be peeled and eaten. Important: it is essential to cut the chestnut shells or else they will burst.

CHESTNUTS IN A PAN
Cut an X into the chestnut shells and (without adding fat) put them in a pan or a tagine. Roast them on a fire with low flames or over the embers, constantly shaking or turning them. They will be done after about 20 minutes.

CHESTNUTS IN A CHESTNUT PAN
In Italy people use a pan with holes to roast the chestnuts over the embers of an indoor fire or over an open fire. Cut an X into the chestnut shells and roast, shaking them continuously.

CALDAROSTE – TUSCAN-STYLE CHESTNUTS
Do not cut the chestnuts. Boil them in a pot of water with bay leaves (2–3 bay leaves for about 500 g/1lb of chestnuts) for about 15 minutes. Strain the chestnuts and leave them to drain; then cut them and roast them in a chestnut pan over the embers. Serve with cheese and red wine or grappa.

Tip
I got this tip from my neighbour who is from Tuscany. Drizzle a little white wine over the freshly roasted chestnuts and leave to marinate in a covered bowl for a few minutes. Then serve while still warm.

SOUTH TYROLEAN CHESTNUTS WITH BACON

Roast the chestnuts in the embers or in a pan over the embers as above. Serve with flatbread (see pages 55, 138 and 185), bacon and a fine red wine.

CHESTNUT RECIPE FROM BRANDENBURG

Peel the chestnuts and carefully scrape off the white skin with a knife. If the skin is brown, you do not need to scrape it off, because it is no longer bitter and the chestnuts will no longer taste furry. Halve the chestnuts and roast in a pan with some olive oil for 10–15 minutes over the embers or low flames. The chestnuts are done when they become slightly glazed and transparent and soft, but not squishy.

CHESTNUT CREAM

Katharina Jahn gave me this delicious chestnut variation. Katharina grew up in Brandenburg in a house that was surrounded by twenty-three chestnut trees. They used to prepare chestnuts in many ways there, but this was her favourite.

Serves 2–3

1 cup chestnuts

4–5 tbsp cream

1 tbsp sugar or honey

1 vanilla pod, split and the seeds scraped out

1 dash rum

Boil the chestnuts in their shells in water for about 30 minutes until they are completely soft. Strain, and remove the shells and skin. Mash the chestnuts with a fork or between two stones. Add the cream, sugar or honey, vanilla and rum to taste and mix thoroughly – a true autumn delicacy.

Tip

Chestnuts often have worms in them. If you put them in water, the wormy ones will float to the top and can easily be removed.

THE LARGE LOAF
A masterpiece of outdoor cuisine

Can you imagine anything more exotic than baking a large loaf of bread on a fire in the middle of the woods?

1 kg (2¼ lb) 7½ cups flour

1 cube fresh yeast or
1 packet dry yeast

about 500 ml (1 pint)
2 cups lukewarm water

1 tsp sugar

2 tsp salt

1 tsp bread seasoning to
taste (e.g. seeds of caraway,
cardamom, fennel, coriander,
nettle or garden angelica)

Put the flour in a bowl and make a well in the middle. Crumble the yeast into this and make a liquid yeast sponge, mixing in some of the water and the sugar. Cover and leave to rest for about 15 minutes. Add the salt and other seasoning and knead into a firm dough with the rest of the water. Cover and leave to rise for 30 minutes in a warm place. Then knead the dough again, make it into a ball and wrap in a kitchen towel.

Cut some branches, 3 cm/1 inch thick, to fit in a large pot and lay them parallel to each other in the bottom of the pot, leaving a space a thick as a finger between each one. Fill the pot with water to about halfway up the branches. Put the dough wrapped in the kitchen towel on top, put on the lid and cook on the fire for about 1 hour. You may need to add some water. Take the bread out, unwrap it and let it cool. The dough will now be shiny. Roast the bread on a grill over the embers, turning it constantly. This will take a further 45 minutes. It should sound hollow when tapped.

Tip
You can add nuts and dry fruit to the dough.

Cooking utensils
A large pot with a lid (you can also make smaller loaves in smaller pots); a grill.

Fire
A fire with flames for cooking the bread and mature embers for baking the loaf.

You can also bake bread according to the pot-in-pot method (see page 72).

PRETZELS
Soft pretzels made the old-fashioned German way

After a long and beautiful day we set up camp by a lake. Our fire was burning nicely, since we were stoking it with beech wood. Some storks were strutting around the clearing. It was already a bit cool that evening; autumn was announcing itself. At the end of the evening, as we let our fire gently burn down, a whitish-grey layer of beech wood ashes covered the fireplace. 'You could make great lye with that,' we thought. Sabine thought of the recipe from her grandmother Mathilde Gerspacher, who still baked pretzels in the traditional way with lye made from beech wood ashes. We decided to try it. We had flour and yeast with us. The next day we had wonderful, warm lye pretzels with our campfire coffee.

Makes 10–12 small pretzels

Lye:

4–5 beech logs or
2 cups beech ashes

2 litres (4¼ pints) 8½ cups water

Dough:

500 g (1 lb) 3¾ cups flour
(wheat or spelt)

1 tsp salt

1 cube fresh yeast or
1 packet dry yeast

2 tbsp coarse salt

water for kneading

Making the lye

Cut shavings out of some of the beech logs and with them light the fire to burn the rest of the logs. The fireplace should contain no ashes from other kinds of wood. When the beech charcoal has smouldered out, let the ashes cool and put them into a cloth bag or cotton sock (no artificial fibres). You need about 2 cups of ashes. Fill the water into an enamel or stainless steel pot (no aluminium, the lye reacts with it), cover and boil. Hang the cloth bag into the boiling water and let it simmer for 3 hours. If you use ready-made potash from the pharmacy, let it boil directly in the water for 3 hours – no need to strain it.

Pretzel dough

Mix the flour and salt. Make a dent in the middle, crumble the yeast into it, pour some lukewarm water on it, stir and dissolve. Cover and let it rise for 15 minutes. Then knead into a dough with the rest of the flour, salt and water, and make a ball. The dough should not stick to your hands.

With your hands, roll the dough into 10–12 strips about 40 cm/1½ ft long; the ends should be as thick as a pencil and the middle about double. Take both ends and form pretzels. Bring the lye without the cloth bag to a boil and carefully let one pretzel after another glide into the water and cook until they float on the surface – this takes about 30 seconds. Take the pretzels out, make a cut along the thick part and sprinkle with coarse salt. Let them rise for another few minutes and then bake fairly hot on a tray in a clay oven or in a Dutch oven until golden brown.

Cooking utensils

An enamel or stainless steel cooking pot, a cotton or linen bag, a surface for rolling the dough (e.g. camping mat, wooden board), a rolling pin (e.g. a debarked branch) and either a grill rack, a clay oven or a Dutch oven for baking.

Fire

Small flames for boiling the lye, strong, mature embers without flames for baking in the Dutch oven, or a well pre-heated clay oven.

ELDERBERRY SOUP
Little Red Riding Hood's favourite

Serves 4

10–15 large heads of elderberries

zest of ½ lemon, unwaxed

½ tsp grated fresh ginger

2 cloves or 3 wild clove roots

about 1 litre (2 pints)
4 cups water

1 tbsp cornflour

4–5 tbsp sugar or honey

Take the berries off the heads and simmer them in a little water with the lemon zest and ginger for 15 minutes. Strain through a seive. Add the remaining water. Mix the cornflour with a little cold water and add to the elderberry juice. Boil, stirring constantly, until the soup has thickened. Sweeten with the sugar or honey.

This soup tastes great hot or cold.

Tip
Serve the soup with semolina dumplings or coconut biscuits soaked in milk.

Cooking utensils
A pot; a bowl or second pot; a sieve or muslin.

Fire
Fire with low flames.

ELDERBERRY PUNCH
Warm and spicy

A delicious, invigorating drink for convivial gatherings around the campfire.

Makes 2–3 beakers of punch

500 g (1 lb) 3¾ cups elderberries, plucked off the heads

250 ml (8½ fl oz) 1 cup water

zest of 1 lemon, unwaxed

½ unwaxed orange, sliced

2 cloves

½ cinnamon stick

¼ litre (8½ fl oz) 1 cup black tea

1 tbsp wild honey

Boil the berries in water for 15 minutes until soft and strain through a sieve or muslin. Add the lemon zest, orange slices and spices and simmer for 10 minutes.

Meanwhile, prepare the black tea. Strain the elderberry juice, mix with the tea and sweeten with the honey. Serve hot.

Cooking utensils
A pot; a bowl or second pot for straining; a sieve or muslin.

Fire
A fire with low flames.

DULCE DE LECHE WITH BARBERRY COMPOTE
A campfire treat

A Russian biologist once told me that he had raised two young orphaned bears with condensed milk and then returned them to the wild. Condensed milk is apparently so nutritious that the bear cubs were healthy and developed marvellously. I use it for a completely different reason, for a feast of a dessert: dulce de leche. Children are crazy about it. Adults prefer this sweet dish with the bittersweet barberry compote. Barberry bushes (Berberis vulgaris) can be found at the edges of woods or in sparse woods. You can gather the scarlet red barberries from August. They stay on the bushes until winter.

Serves 4

1 200 ml (6¾ fl oz) can sweetened condensed milk (Russian condensed milk is best: it is available in Russian food stores)

2 cups freshly picked barberries (or dried ones, available in Turkish or Middle Eastern food shops) or dried cranberries

½ cup sugar or honey

100 ml (4 fl oz) ½ cup water

Simmer the unopened can of condensed milk in a pot of water for 2 hours. Take it out and let it cool in cold water for about 30 minutes; then open it. The condensed milk should have turned into a light brown caramel cream. Scoop this out with a spoon.

Meanwhile, simmer the barberries with the sugar or honey and water for 30 minutes, stirring constantly. If necessary sweeten more. Serve with the caramel cream. The sweet cream complements the bittersweet flavour of the barberries and makes a wonderful dessert at a campfire.

Caution
Do not put the unopened can in the fire or the embers, as it might explode.

Cooking utensils
Two pots; can opener.

Fire
Fire with low flames.

ANGELICA BOATS
A poem to autumn

On an autumn hiking trip to the Kleinwalsertal Valley (between Austria and Germany) we picked lingonberries in a sunny place close to the summit. When we were coming down, we found some majestic angelica plants in a damp clearing. Their dry stems were particularly thick. We still had some chocolate in our provisions. All these combined resulted in these delicious angelica boats: a poem to autumn made of gently melting dark chocolate with the aroma of the wild, proud angelica plant and the bittersweet berries.

1 firm angelica stem, fresh or dried, 10–20 cm/4–8 inches long, with a transverse partition in the stem at both ends, or several smaller stems

100 g (3½ oz) ½ cup high-quality dark chocolate for melting

2–3 tbsp fresh or dried wild berries (e.g. lingonberries, blueberries, barberries)

Cut the hollow angelica stem in half lengthwise, so that you have two oblong, boat-shaped bowls.

Break the chocolate into pieces. Melt it in a pot, glass or beaker in a bain-marie on the embers.

Place the angelica bowls so that they will not tip over, distribute the berries between them and pour the melted chocolate over the berries. Let them set in a cool place. Take out each chocolate bar by easing the long side of the stem away from it and or turning the boat upside down on to a surface.

Cooking utensils
A pot to hold the water for the bain-marie; a smaller pot or beaker to go inside it.

Fire
A small fire with low flames or embers.

Wild plant information
You can find thick stems of wild angelica (Angelica sylvestris) or garden angelica (A. archangelica) in wet grassland and alluvial forests up to an altitude of 1,700 m/5,577 ft. Caution: angelica can easily be confused with giant hogweed or other umbellifers. Giant hogweed can lead to severe skin irritations when exposed to direct sunlight. Gather the plant only if you are entirely sure you have the right one. Alternatively you can use the stems of Japanese knotweed.

WINTER

Time seems to stand still. Jack Frost has laid his chill blanket over the countryside. But if you can light a fire outside, and prepare something warm over it to eat and drink, you can put your trust in Nature and enjoy the winter tranquillity. No other season brings home to us so poignantly that fire is life itself.

BERNESE RÖSTI
Crispy potatoes at a warm fire

1 kg (2¼ lb) waxy potatoes

3 tbsp clarified butter or vegetable oil

salt and pepper

Boil the potatoes until al dente and let them cool (you could do this at home and bring the pre-cooked potatoes with you). Peel the potatoes and coarsely grate them. Heat the clarified butter or oil in a pan, add the grated potatoes and press flat until the potatoes evenly cover the bottom of the pan.

Fry until the bottom is golden brown and firm like a cake. Turn the rösti with the help of a flat lid, plate or wooden board and fry the other side until golden brown and crispy. Season with salt and pepper. Important: be sure to use enough fat, as the rösti can easily burn otherwise. Serve hot.

You can make one big rösti or several small ones in one pan.

Variations
- Fry some diced bacon in a pan and mix it into the grated potatoes.
- Serve the rösti with a fried egg on top.
- Put a slice of cheese on the rösti, place a lid on the pan and let the cheese melt.
- In summer you can add wild herbs such as thyme, marjoram or caraway.

Tips
You can also make rösti with raw potatoes. Gently squeeze out the water from the grated potatoes with a piece of muslin before frying. Rösti made with raw potatoes takes about 10 minutes longer to fry.

Bernese rösti is traditionally made with cooked potatoes, while raw potatoes are preferred in Zurich and western Switzerland.

Cooking utensils
A pan (e.g. cast iron); perhaps another pan for eggs and/or bacon; a grater; a lid, plate or wooden board; a wooden spatula (perhaps carved out of a branch).

Fire
A small young fire with flames that are not too high.

On a clear winter morning, Silvia saddled her horse, Sandy, packed various cooking utensils and some logs in her saddlebags and rode off. After a nice long ride in the December snow, she stopped at the edge of a forest. She lit a fire, settled down on her warm saddle blanket and made a cowgirl breakfast on the gently crackling fire. The smell of spiced tea, rösti and bacon combined with the balsamic scent of the warming fire and the magic of the snowy landscape – what a precious moment in this winter wonderland!

A cowgirl breakfast can consist of any or all of the following: Bernese rösti, fried eggs, bannocks, pancakes and chai or campfire coffee.

CHAI
Indian spiced tea

I got to know and love chai during my time in India. Despite the hot weather there, the spiced tea had a stimulating and strengthening effect. Later, when I was trekking in Nepal, I appreciated this delicious drink again: it warmed not only my cold fingers but also my entire body, and gave me strength for the mountain trek. The milk for the drink had been taken from a water buffalo shortly before and gave the chai a particularly creamy flavour. Instead of water buffalo milk I like to add a dash of cream to my chai. As soon as winter starts, I drink my chai with galangal root to prevent colds.

1½ litres (3 pints) 6⅓ cups water

½ cinnamon stick

2 cardamom pods, squashed

1 slice fresh ginger, about ½ cm thick

2 cloves

1 generous tbsp black tea leaves (Darjeeling or English tea)

2 tbsp sugar

150 ml (5 fl oz) ¾ cup milk or milk–cream mixture

Put the cold water and the spices in a pot with a lid. Bring to a boil and simmer for about 10 minutes. Add the tea leaves and sugar and simmer without the lid for a further 2–3 minutes; if necessary, stir until the sugar has dissolved. Finally, add the milk and bring to a boil. Strain and drink hot.

Tip
Instead of ginger you could use galangal root (also called laos and available in Asian food shops). Both ginger and galangal root stimulate the body's defence mechanisms, protecting it from colds and flu.

Cooking utensils
Either a pot with a lid or a hobo oven; a sieve.

Fire
Fire with low flames or a Swedish log fire.

PANCAKES
Comfort food for outdoors

On a canoe trip in eastern Poland, we purchased some fresh eggs from a local farmer. The only shop in the village offered little in the way of food, except for beer. What a stroke of luck, though – because that is how this recipe for Polish pancakes originated. It has become legendary and has often served as comfort food on a cold or rainy day on a wilderness trip.

400 g (14 oz) 3 cups flour

4 eggs

400 ml (13½ fl oz) 1¾ cups milk

1 pinch salt

⅛ litre (4¼ fl oz) ½ cup beer (e.g. dark wheat beer) or 1 tsp baking powder and a little water

oil, clarified butter or butter for frying

Mix all the ingredients into a batter. Cover and leave to rest for 30 minutes. Heat the oil, clarified butter or butter in a pan and bake individual pancakes in it. Serve with maple syrup, Fir Tree Syrup (see page 173) or hot wild berry compote.

Variation
Sprinkle some blueberries or elderberries into the pancake, fold and flip the pancake and brown for about 1 more minute.

Tip
The pancakes taste best when prepared in a cast iron pan.

Cooking utensils
A pan or the flat lid of a Dutch oven; a wooden spatula.

Fire
A small fire with low flames.

BAKED APPLES WITH FIR TREE SYRUP
Home sweet woods

Fir tree syrup:

2 handfuls fresh fir twig tips, chopped, and perhaps also twigs of Douglas fir or spruce (caution: do not use yew, as it is poisonous)

½ lemon, sliced

1½ litres (3 pints) 6⅓ cups water

1 kg (2¼ lb) 5¼ cups sugar (or 250 g (½ lb) 1⅓ cups gelling sugar 1:4)

4 apples ('Boskoop' apples are especially suitable)

butter or oil for greasing

syrup

In a pot, steep the fir twig tips and the lemon slices in the water. Heat and simmer for about 30 minutes, and then strain. Boil the water and sugar down to a syrup.

Put the apples on the greased bottom of a Dutch oven. Place the Dutch oven in the embers and cover the lid with embers. (Instead of a Dutch oven you could use the pot-in-pot method: see page 72.)

After about 15 minutes, carefully lift the lid and check the consistency of the apples. They will be done when the skin pops open slightly.

Pour the warm syrup over the apples, leave to infuse for a couple of minutes and serve hot.

Tip
To prepare without a pot, simply place the apples on a stone on the edge of the fire with a lot of embers and very few flames, and occasionally turn them so that they are cooked from all sides and the inside is soft.

Variations
Cut a lid off the apples, remove the core and fill them – e.g. with marzipan, red currant jam, nuts, candied ginger or wild fruit such as barberries or blueberries. You could also sprinkle some cinnamon inside the apples. Replace the lid and prepare as above.

Or cook the apples, filled or unfilled, in a pot as above, but instead of water use 500 ml (1 pint) 2 cups of port wine with 1 slice of fresh ginger and 4 tbsp of wild honey.

Cooking utensils
A Dutch oven or a pot in a larger pot (put the smaller pot on a sand and gravel mixture in the larger pot; see Little Red Riding Hood's Bundt Cake, page 72).

Fire
A mature fire with small flames for the syrup and sufficient embers for the Dutch oven.

BANNOCKS
Native American bread in a pan

This recipe comes from my Native American friend Shirley. She lives in the Yukon Territory in north-western Canada. Bannocks are part of every social gathering there; that is why the recipe is for fifteen people. If your 'tribe' is smaller, you can halve the quantities.

Makes about 30

1 kg (2¼ lb) 7½ cups flour

1 tsp baking powder

2 level tbsp salt

1 tbsp sugar (brown)

about ¾ litre (1½ pints)
3 cups cold water

about 500 ml (1 pint)
2 cups vegetable oil (e.g.
sunflower oil, rapeseed oil) for
deep-frying

Mix all the ingredients into a dough and use immediately. Heat some oil in a pan. With a large spoon, take some dough, put it in the pan and press it flat to a diameter of about 5 cm/2 inches. When the bottom of the bread has browned a little, turn it with a fork and brown the other side. The bannocks will be done when you flick them with your finger and they sound hollow. Serve hot.

Variations

There are countless variations.
- In Canada they put cranberries in the dough. You could also use other wild berries such as blueberries, barberries or lingonberries.
- Some recipes use milk or powdered milk in the dough.
- Other possible ingredients include: raisins, grated coconut, pieces of dried apple, beechnuts, pine seeds, small pieces of cheese and bacon.
- You can also add wild herbs to the dough.

Bannocks make great breakfast food at campfires, and they also taste good as a side dish with stews and meat.

Cooking utensils

A cast iron pan or the flat lid of a Dutch oven. You can also make bannocks on a hot stone, a roof tile or a muurikka.

Fire

A mature fire with low flames for constant heat.

PÖRKÖLT
The classic goulash

This rustic and tasty goulash is a great dish to satisfy a sizeable group at a campfire. The preparation leaves enough time for chatting, storytelling and wine tasting while the goulash simmers. Uli Hallerberg was given this recipe twenty years ago by a Hungarian farmer's wife and has now passed it on to me.

Serves 8–10

sunflower oil for frying

½ kg (1 lb) 3⅓ cups onions, diced

garlic to taste, diced

½ kg (1 lb) 3⅓ cups long peppers, some of them the hot green variety, pitted and cut into rings

1 kg (2¼ lb) 6½ cups tomatoes, diced

1½ kg (3⅓ lb) 7 cups beef, diced

1½ kg (3⅓ lb) 7 cups pork, diced

salt and pepper

½ litre (1 pint) 2 cups red wine

4 heaped tbsp paprika

Heat some oil in a pot and braise the onions and garlic in it. Add the peppers and tomatoes and briefly fry. Add the diced beef and leave to simmer for 1 hour while occasionally adding water so that there is always enough liquid in the pot. Now add the pork and simmer for another hour. Season with salt and pepper, and towards the end add the red wine. Right at the end sprinkle in the paprika. It is important that neither the paprika nor the red wine get too hot; otherwise the goulash will taste bitter. Keep stirring occasionally throughout the cooking process. At the end, the meat should be very tender and the vegetables boiled down almost to a smooth gravy.

Serve with baked or toasted bread and, of course, red wine.

Tip

Pörkölt tastes even better when it is re-heated – so, if you can keep it in a fridge or freezer, make a larger quantity and keep some for another occasion.

Cooking utensils

A large pot or Hungarian pökölt pot with a tripod.

Fire

A fire with constant flames for slow cooking (for several hours).

CHILLI WITH SOY
A spicy treat

Serves 4

700 ml (1½ pints) 3 cups vegetable stock

250 g (½ lb) 1⅓ cups dried soy, finely diced (from a health food shop)

1 large onion, diced

2 garlic cloves, finely chopped

1–2 tbsp olive oil

2 red peppers, pitted, diced

3 carrots, sliced

2 cans tomatoes, strained

1 can peeled tomatoes

2 cans kidney beans

chilli powder, pepper, salt and oregano

Bring the vegetable stock to a boil in a large pot. Take it off the fire, stir in the diced soy and allow it to soak for 10 minutes. (The pot should be large enough to allow the soy to swell to three times its original volume.) Strain through a sieve or muslin.

Lightly fry the onion and garlic in the pot in olive oil, add the diced soy and briefly sear. Add the peppers and carrots and continue frying. Add the strained and peeled tomatoes and kidney beans and simmer for 15 minutes. Season with the spices. Serve with toasted bread.

Tips

This is a vegetarian version of chilli con carne. Since minced meat needs to be kept cool and is therefore not so easy to take camping, diced soy is a great alternative. It keeps and is very light. Even die-hard meat eaters like this 'chilli con soy'.

If you leave out the kidney beans this recipe makes a great Bolognese sauce for pasta.

Variation

Soak 250 g (½ lb) 1⅓ cups dried kidney beans in water overnight and increase the cooking time to 30–40 minutes. That way you can forget about the can opener and cans and your luggage will be a lot lighter.

Cooking utensils

A large pot; a sieve or muslin; perhaps a can opener.

Fire

A constantly burning fire with flames that are not too high.

BORSCHT
Winter Stew

Borscht, a winter stew, has a long tradition in Russia and Ukraine. This hearty dish is wonderful for a cold winter evening at a campfire. There are countless variations of borscht, so you can vary the recipe according to your taste and your mood. I brought my recipe back from a tavern in the woods of Bialowieza in eastern Poland, on the Russian border. Every time I prepare it, I think of that ancient forest, the wild bison there and the evenings we spent at the crackling fire.

Serves 6–8

500 g (1 lb) beef (brisket)

about 3 litres (6 pints)
12 cups water

3 beetroots, uncooked

1 bay leaf

3 potatoes

2 parsley roots

2 onions

2 carrots

1 red pepper, pitted

3 tomatoes, skinned, pulp removed and quartered

oil for frying (e.g. sunflower oil)

½ medium white cabbage

2 cups green beans, cut into pieces

salt and pepper

1½ cups sour cream or crème fraîche (or smetana, fatty sour cream from a Russian food shop)

Put the meat (in one piece) in a pot with water, bring to a boil and simmer for a while. If there is foam on the surface, skim it off. Add the beetroots (whole and peeled), some salt and the bay leaf and simmer for about 1 hour.

Meanwhile, prepare the vegetables. Cut the potatoes and parsley roots into strips or slices. Quarter the onions, slice the carrots and cut the peppers into strips. Heat some oil in a pan and add the vegetables gradually (the onions first, the tomatoes last) and fry for about 10 minutes.

Cut the cabbage into fine strips and boil in a separate pot with the green beans for 10–15 minutes and then strain.

Add all the vegetables to the meat, cover and simmer for another hour. Take out the beetroot and the meat, cut them into small pieces and return to the soup. If the borscht is too thick at this point, add some water. Bring to a boil, season with salt and pepper and serve hot.

Put a generous dollop of sour cream or crème fraîche on each portion of soup and, if available, sprinkle some freshly chopped dill over it. Serve with fresh bread or blinis – and vodka as desired.

Tip
Borscht tastes even better when you warm it up the next day.

Cooking utensils
A large pot; a smaller pot; a pan.

Fire
A fire with low flames for constant heat.

RUSSIAN HOGWEED SOUP
A fortifying broth

1 onion, diced

oil for frying

1 large potato, diced

1 carrot, cut into thick sticks

about 1 litre (2 pints) 4 cups water or vegetable stock

2 cups freshly cut young hogweed leaves (also young stems)

½ cup finely chopped sorrel leaves

salt and pepper

other herbs and spices as desired (e.g. cayenne pepper, nutmeg, lovage, marjoram)

Lightly fry the onion in hot oil. Add the potato and carrot and fry for another couple of minutes. Add the herbs and spices and the water or vegetable stock and boil until soft. Add the hogweed and sorrel leaves and simmer for another 4–5 minutes. Season with salt and pepper. Serve with a dollop of sour cream or crème fraîche, as desired.

Tip

Hogweed can cause skin irritation on sensitive skin in direct sunlight. There are similar poisonous plants in the family of the common hogweed, so gather this plant only if you are entirely sure you can tell them apart. You can easily grow hogweed in your garden. It self-seeds and requires no weeding.

Cooking utensils and fire
As for Borscht (page 178).

Common hogweed is the forefather of borscht. The name borscht is apparently derived from an old Slavic word for common hogweed (*Heracleum sphondylium*). This umbellifer, which grows on the edges of meadows and paths in central Europe, was at one time commonly used for cooking. It is still occasionally added to borscht, instead of or together with sorrel. Tender young hogweed leaves are ideal for salad or dumpling fillings (see pages 100–1) as well as for vegetable stock, adding a chicken stock flavour. The stems and the still-folded leaves are most full of flavour when gathered before flowering. Caution: do not confuse hogweed with the noxious giant hogweed, which is much bigger and has red dots on its hairy stems.

BLINIS
Food to go

Makes 15–20 blinis

¼ cube fresh yeast or
1 tsp dry yeast

1–1½ cups lukewarm milk

1 tbsp sugar

1 tsp salt

1 tbsp butter, melted

125 g (4 oz) 1 cup buckwheat
flour

vegetable oil for frying

butter, crème fraîche or sour
cream for spreading

Dissolve the yeast in the milk. Add the other ingredients and mix into a liquid batter. Cover and leave to stand in a warm place for 30 minutes. Then thoroughly mix again so that the batter is aerated and makes small bubbles.

Heat some oil in a pan. Put 1 tbsp of batter per blini in the pan and spread each one flat to a diameter of about 5 cm/2 inches. Fry until golden brown on both sides. Spread butter, crème fraîche or sour cream on top and serve hot. If you wish, you can sprinkle them with fresh dill or fennel, chopped spring onions, chives or wild herbs such as wild garlic, watercress or garlic mustard.

Tips

Blinis are sometimes prepared with beaten egg whites or whipped cream. However, this recipe has been kept as simple as possible, so that it is easy to prepare on a hike or canoeing trip on an open fire. The blinis are still delicious in this simple version.

In Russia, blinis are made in a cast iron pan, which has previously been greased with half an onion dipped in oil. Traditionally they are served spread with crème fraîche or butter, and with caviar or salmon on top. They also taste great with a sweet topping such as berry compote or jam.

Cooking utensils

A pan, muurikka or hot stone.

Fire

A small fire with low flames; embers for the hot stone.

Blinis (or blintzes) are said to have been a pre-Christian ritual food symbolizing the return of the sun after a long winter, like the round yellow Easter flatbread made in other countries.

ONION SOUP
A treat for the palate

This hearty onion soup is perfect for an autumn or winter evening by the fire. During a workshop in winter when there was a lot of snow, we made snowshoes out of natural materials. Towards evening we sat round the campfire and enjoyed a delicious onion soup which Carola had made for us. Since then onion soup has been my idea of a wonderful way to round off a beautiful winter day with friends at a campfire.

Serves 6–8

1 tbsp butter

2 tbsp olive oil

7–8 large onions, halved and cut into fine slices

2 tbsp flour

2 litres (3½ pints) 8½ cups stock (beef or vegetable)

200 ml (½ pint) ¾ cup dry white wine

3 tbsp cognac or other brandy

salt and pepper

Heat the butter and oil in a large pot and fry the onions until golden brown; keep scraping the onions off the bottom so that they do not burn. The slow frying lets the onions develop their sweet aroma. Sprinkle on the flour and keep frying. Then add the stock, white wine and cognac, and simmer for 30–40 minutes, stirring occasionally. Season with salt and pepper.

Tip

Serve with toasted white bread slices, focaccia, blinis or flatbread with a slice of melted cheese on top, or with sage tempura.

Cooking utensils

A large pot; a grill rack or hot stone for toasting the bread with cheese.

Fire

A fire with lower flames for constant heat.

BREAD ON A STICK WITH BACON

You can also serve onion soup with this bread.

Prepare a pizza dough (see Pizza Calzone, page 49). Make strips as thick as a finger and about 20 cm/8 inches long and wrap each one in one or two long slices of bacon. Wind the strips with the bacon around wooden skewers and bake over the embers, turning them constantly.

DAAL BAHT
A traditional Indian dish

Serves 4

300 g (10½ oz) 1½ cups red or
yellow split lentils (daal)

about 1 litre (2 pints)
4 cups water

1 tbsp clarified butter,(or ghee,
available in Asian food shops)

1 tsp curcuma powder

¼ tsp cayenne pepper

1 tsp cumin

4 whole cloves

1 tsp mustard

1 tsp salt

Boil the lentils in a pot with the water for 20–30 minutes until soft.

In a smaller pot or pan, heat the clarified butter and fry the spices in it for a few minutes, stirring constantly. Add to the cooked lentils and simmer for a few more minutes.

Serve with rice, vegetables and poppadoms or Chapatti (see page 185).

Tips
These lentils are particularly suitable for cooking outdoors because they are quick to cook.

If you add some more water during cooking you will get a tasty warm soup. Instead of the spices you could use 1 tsp of ready-made curry powder (such as dal masala from an Asian food shop).

Cooking utensils
A pot or hobo oven; a small pot or pan.

Fire
A small fire with lower flames.

CHAPATTI
Indian flatbread

Makes 7–8 chapatti

250 g (½ lb) 2 cups flour

1 tsp salt

about 250 ml (8½ fl oz)
1 cup water

or:

125 g (4 oz) 1 cup
wholemeal flour

125 g (4 oz) 1 cup plain flour

1 tsp salt

2 tbsp clarified butter or ghee
(available in Asian food shops)

about 1 cup hot but
not boiling water

Knead the flour, salt and water into a smooth dough. Or with the alternative ingredients, first knead the ghee into the flour, and then gradually add the water, while constantly kneading with the other hand.

Roll the dough into a thick sausage and divide it into 7–8 portions, rolling each one out to the size of a plate.

Heat a hot stone, a clay slab, a muurikka, the lid of a metal barrel or a large pan. Do not grease. Lay the chapatti on it and bake on both sides for 2–3 minutes. They will make bubbles and inflate.

Or you can bake them in the hot ashes of a fire, covering them with ashes. The dough should be slightly dryer so that as little ash as possible sticks to the bread.

Cooking utensils
A hot stone, a pan, a clay slab or a muurikka; or bake in hot ashes.

Fire
According to the choice of cooking utensils.

In the small ashram in the north of India where I learned yoga, our yoga teacher and master Swami Prakesh Bharti insisted on cooking for his students every day. To him, healthy food was the basis for a healthy and good life. He always served chapatti with the various vegetable dishes he prepared, with freshly pestled curry pastes. He baked the chapatti on a flat round metal plate over a small fire. When I make chapatti today, the smell takes me back to the friendly atmosphere at that fire with my yoga teacher in Rishikesh.

CARMEN'S GINGER-COCONUT SOUP
An exotic dish to warm you up

Serves 4

4 sticks celery

2 shallots

1 garlic clove

1 piece fresh ginger, about
2 cm/¾ inch, peeled

2 tbsp sunflower oil

1 leek

2 carrots

50 g (1¼ oz) ¼ cup basmati rice

50 g (1¼ oz) ¼ cup scented rice

1 tsp turmeric powder

1¼ litre (2½ pints) 5¼ cups
vegetable stock

about 400 ml (13½ fl oz)
1¾ cups coconut milk (packet or can)

Finely dice the celery, shallots, garlic and ginger and lightly fry in the oil. Cut the leek and carrots into fine strips and add to the pan. Add both kinds of rice and fry until the rice is transparent. Add the turmeric, vegetable stock and coconut milk and simmer for 10 minutes. If necessary, season with salt.

Tip

This is a quick and delicious vegetarian dish for which you need to take very few ingredients with you. It warms you up on a cold winter day, so it is ideal for a snowshoe trek or a cross-country skiing excursion.

Cooking utensils

A pot or hobo oven.

Fire

A small fire with medium flames.

POPPADOMS
Delicious nibbles

Poppadoms are ideal for the outdoor kitchen because they keep for a long time and can therefore be taken on any excursion. This thin flatbread can be prepared in two ways: either on a grill or in a pan; or you can bake them without a grill or a pan by using on a hot flat stone in the embers. They are an excellent accompaniment, for instance to Indian rice dishes, dahl or soups, and they make a delicious snack.

ready-made poppadoms
(Indian flatbread),
from an Asian food shop

vegetable oil for cooking in a pan

On a grill
Put the poppadoms on a grill over a fire with a lot of hot embers. After about 30 seconds, the bottoms will become transparent and crispy brown, and they will expand. Turn the poppadoms with tongs and bake on the other side. Caution: they burn easily.

In a pan
Heat a little oil in a pan. Put the poppadoms into the pan. After a short time they will expand and become golden brown. Take them out immediately. Usually they do not have to be turned and baked on the other side.

Cooking utensils
A pan or a grill; or a hot stone.

Fire
For grilling: mature embers with low flames. For baking in a pan: a fire with small flames. For cooking on a hot stone: a fire with a lot of embers.

I discovered these wonderfully crispy, spicy, paper-thin treats in India, where they play an essential part in traditional cuisine. They are made there with urad flour, and sometimes also with rice flour and spices; they are some of the few ready-made products there. Poppadoms are available with different spice varieties.

ZUPPA DI FARRO
A friendly soup

This tasty soup requires very few ingredients and little cooking experience, and it always turns out well – it is a truly 'friendly' soup.

Serves 4

200 g (7 oz) 1½ cups spelt (or wild emmer) grains, whole

oil for frying

2 onions, finely chopped

1 garlic clove, finely chopped

2 carrots, diced

3–4 celery sticks, diced

about 1 litre (2 pints) 4 cups vegetable stock

salt and pepper

extra virgin olive oil to drizzle on top

Soak the spelt or emmer grains in plenty of water the night before. The next day, boil in fresh water for about 20 minutes and strain. Lightly fry the vegetables in hot oil in a pot. Add the spelt, fill the pot up with vegetable stock and boil for about 1 hour. Season with salt and pepper. Drizzle with extra virgin olive oil before serving.

Serve with toasted bread, flatbread, Bread on a Stick with Bacon (see page 183) or Sourdough Pancakes (see page 122).

Cooking utensils
A pot or hobo oven; perhaps a sieve for straining.

Fire
A fire with low flames for constant heat.

Wild plant information
You can flavour the soup by boiling it with sprigs of rosemary or the leaves of wild herbs such as thyme, marjoram, common hogweed or watercress.

TARTES FLAMBÉES
A sure success

Makes about 10 tartes
flambées or pizzas

500 g (1 lb) 4 cups flour

1 packet dry yeast or
1 cube fresh yeast

1 tsp sugar

½ tsp salt

4 tbsp oil

250–300 ml (½–¾ pint)
1–1¼ cup water

Topping:

3 cups crème fraîche
or sour cream

2–3 onions, cut into thin rings

about 100 g (3½ oz) ½ cup
bacon, diced or sliced

pepper

In a bowl, mix the flour and the dry yeast well. Add the sugar, salt, oil and water and knead. If you use fresh yeast, proceed as with the pizza dough on page 142. Only add water until the dough does not stick to the bowl. Cover and leave to rise close to the fire for about 1 hour. Then knead again.

Roll the dough out into thin pizzas. Spread crème fraîche on each one, put the onion rings and bacon on top and season with pepper. Grease the Dutch oven, and lay a pizza inside, one after the other. Place the Dutch oven in the embers and cover the lid with plenty of embers. Bake for 5–10 minutes. Cook the remaining pizzas, one after the other.

Variations
For vegetarian tartes flambées, leave out the bacon; use instead finely chopped leek, thinly sliced raw potatoes or pre-boiled, finely chopped, peeled pumpkin. You can add herbs such as rosemary, thyme, marjoram, oregano or caraway. Instead of crème fraîche you could use crumbled feta cheese.

Cooking utensils
A Dutch oven; a bowl; a bottle (to use as a rolling pin).

Fire
A mature fire with a lot of embers and few flames.

CHEESE FONDUE
From the Swiss mountains

A cheese fondue creates a convivial atmosphere at a campfire. And what happens if someone loses their bread in the pot? You can make up your own rules. They don't need to impose the dramatic forfeits that were inflicted in 'Asterix in Switzerland' . . .

Serves 4

1 garlic clove, halved

400 g (14 oz) 3¼ cup Gruyère cheese, finely grated

400 g (14 oz) 3¼ cup Vacherin cheese from Fribourg (alternatively Emmental or Appenzeller cheese)

350 ml (²/₃ pint) 1½ cups dry white wine

1–2 tsp lemon juice

2 tsp cornflour

20–30 ml (²/₃ fl oz) 1½ tbsp kirschwasser or brandy

freshly ground pepper and nutmeg

500 g (1 lb) 4 cups white bread, cut into bite-size cubes

Rub the inside of the fondue pot with the garlic clove. Put the cheese, white wine and lemon juice into the pot. Mix the cornflour with the kirschwasser and add. Slowly melt the cheese on low heat stirring constantly until creamy.

Season with pepper and nutmeg. Then do not put any more logs on the fire; just keep the fondue warm with the embers.

Thread the bread cubes on wooden skewers, dip them in the cheese fondue and enjoy while hot.

Tip
When you are on the move, you may want to take ready-made fondue with you (high-quality products are available in supermarkets or cheese shops). Simply heat in a pot or a hobo oven, stirring constantly, until the mixture is creamy.

Cooking utensils
A fondue pot (caquelon), an enamel or clay pot, a hobo oven or a Dutch oven; wooden skewers.

Fire
A mature fire with low flames and embers.

ALPINE RACLETTE
Rustic food for herdsmen

This wonderful alpine dish is ideal for autumn or winter evenings at campfires or at an indoor fireside. The smell of the creamy melting cheese and the fire inspire stories about mountain trolls, fairies, marmots and mountain ghosts.

The dish is said to have originated in the Valais mountains in Switzerland. The alpine herdsmen there had plenty of cheese and a healthy appetite, which were probably the inspiration for this recipe. In her famous children's book Heidi, Johanna Spyri describes how Heidi's grandfather 'fries cheese on a skewer' on the fire.

To aid digestion, you might want to finish off with a schnapps . . .

¼–½ wheel of full-fat cheese for melting (e.g. raclette cheese, Gryuère or cheese from Goms or Valais), about 200 g (7 oz) 1½ cups per person

Serve with:

potatoes with skins

pickled gherkins

pickled onions

Put the cheese on a flat stone as close to the fire as possible, so that the side closest to the fire starts to melt. With a large knife or wooden spatula, scrape the melted cheese directly on to roasted slices of bread, plates or small wooden boards.

Serve with boiled or baked potatoes, pickled gherkins and pickled onions.

Cooking utensils
A flat stone; a knife or wooden spatula (carved out of a log or branch).

Fire
A mature fire with a bed of embers on one side for melting the cheese.

KRAMBAMBULI PUNCH
Punch without a pot, grill or fire

When I first had this drink on a snowshoe hike, my black dog was with us. In the glow of the fire, and inspired by my dog, one of us told the story of Krambambuli the dog, who was sold for twelve bottles of cherry brandy (taken from the story by Marie von Ebner-Eschenbach). Since then this fiery punch, prepared without a pot, has been called krambambuli. It's great for a snowshoe hike by full moon or à deux on a park bench in the snow . . .

Put some home-made mulled wine in a thermos. Pour into porcelain or metal mugs. Slice a large orange and put a slice on each mug. Pile two brown sugar cubes on each orange slice. Drench the sugar with rum and set alight.

'Think about what really counts in life, because nobody says at the end: "I should have spent more time in the office."'
Eckart von Hirschhausen (German physician and comedian)

FIR-TREE PUNCH
A recipe for the forest bar

1 litre (2 pints) 4 cups water

1 slice fresh ginger

¼ unwaxed lemon

1 handful dried apple rings

1 tbsp sugar

2 handfuls chopped fir or douglas fir twig tips (caution: do not use yew or shinglewood as they are poisonous)

Bring the water to a boil with the ginger, lemon, apple rings and sugar. Add the fir twigs, cover and simmer over the embers for 10–15 minutes. Strain and drink hot.

Tip
You can also use spruce or pine twigs, although the drink tastes best with fir or Douglas fir twigs. Take only a limited amount of twigs from each tree, to protect them.

Cooking utensils
A pot.

Fire
A small fire with medium flames and sufficient embers for keeping the drink warm, or a Swedish log fire.

ANCIENT ROMAN MEAD
An antique sundowner

This is a delicious drink to warm you up in winter. The recipe is from Apicius, a collector of recipes writing in the first century AD.

250 g (½ lb) ¾ cup acacia honey

2 750-ml (1½-pint) bottles retsina (Greek resinated wine) or 2 bottles white wine and a walnut-sized piece of pine resin

5 fresh or dried dates, finely chopped

4 bay leaves

15 peppercorns, coarsely pestled

10–15 saffron threads (not powder)

Heat the honey in a pot on a low heat. Stir in the wine, heat and stir the simmering liquid well. Remove from the fire and skim the foam off the surface with a spoon.

Add the dates and spices and simmer for about 10 minutes, stirring continuously. Strain and serve.

Cooking utensils
A pot; a spoon or straining ladle; perhaps a sieve.

Fire
Moderate fire with small flames and with plenty of embers for keeping the drink warm, or a Swedish log fire

A WARM THANK YOU

It is said that 'Whoever lights a fire and cooks on it will never be alone for long.' This is what I experienced when I was working on this book, to which I dedicated an entire year. I was surrounded by helpful and inspiring people, without whom this book would never have turned out as it has.

The person who laid the foundation for my love of cooking was my mother, a great cook and the best host in the world, and the two cooks Luise Theurer and Helga Lambert, who spoiled me with their Swabian cuisine. The numerous cooks I met on my travels, who shared their recipes with me and let me look into their pots, stimulated my interest in culinary experiences.

For my knowledge of fire I have to thank my joy in playing with fire and my wilderness teachers: Sun Bear, Owl Woman, Frank Red, Hawk, Tom Brown and Jon Young.

Carmen Meyer supported me actively and with much dedication at my 'wilderness desk', writing the text and recipes and acquiring material.

Angelika Weigand and Anne Gärtner cast a critical eye over my manuscript and contributed many useful points. Sabine Pohl checked the recipes, using her extensive knowledge on food. My best and most critical recipe tester was my son Silvano, who also helped me with the book in many other ways.

Hannes Kostron, Anne Gärtner, Berko Schröder, Klaus Serda, Alexandra Como and Tina Schneider, with their extensive expertise, contagious enthusiasm and extraordinary dedication, helped me a great deal with the food styling, cooked confidently on the fire and made the gadgets we needed.

Recipes were contributed by: Rainer Besser, Tina Schneider, Wulf Hain, Christoph Freese, Aunt Tessi, Uncle Andreas, Sabine Pohl, Shirley Lord, Kalani Souza, Ulrich Hallerberg, Katia Leonardo, Adrienne Marti, Hans-Jörg Streit and Markus Stöckle.

Additional photographs came from: Silvano Rizzi, Eva Köllner, Carmen Meyer, Rokhaya N'diaye, Conny Striegel, Martin Folgmann, Yasmin Oparango, Niklas Köllner, the Frei family, Silvia Rettenmaier, Frank Schanz, Shirley Lord, Peter Speiser, Stefan Schmid, Felix and Laura Schmid, Eva Pracht, Oliver Stapelfeld and Sabrina Martl.

The children at the birthday party and under the umbrella on pages 69–71 are: Xaver Virnekäs, Anton Virnekäs, Kaspar Virnekäs, Emil Matias, Emma Hofmeister, Paula Tröster, Alexandra Prause, Ida Mader and Tino Mader.

Some of our models were animals: Lucy, Jack, Ben, Sandy and Hildegard.

Profesor Günther Eberl provided his kayak, Katia Frei wove the wicker mesh and Madfred Lip arranged the barrel.

To ensure that this book would be not only a treat for the taste buds but also a feast for the eyes, photographers Ulrike Schmid and Sabine Mader took beautiful pictures throughout the year with great dedication.

My warmest thanks to everybody.

ABOUT THE AUTHOR AND PHOTOGRAPHERS

Susanne Fischer-Rizzi

Traditional healer, herbal expert and outdoor specialist, she is a lecturer at ARVEN, her school for medicinal plants, aromatherapy and wilderness wisdom, and has been imparting her knowledge in seminars, workshops and lectures for over thirty years. She is passionate about cooking on an open fire and has acquire a wide experience in this art on the countless wilderness seminars she has led. So far she has published twelve very successful books which have been translated into many languages.

Sabine Mader and Ulrike Schmid

Photographers Sabine Mader and Ulrike Schmid have been working as a successful creative team for years. Together they run the Fotos mit Geschmack (Photos with Taste) studio in Alling, Upper Bavaria. On journeys, in the countryside and in the studio, they focus on their passion: food. They work for distinguished agencies and publishers, and their cookery books have received many awards. They spent a year on the road for this book, always outdoors, at the open fire and in challenging weather and lighting conditions.

www.fotos-mitgeschmack.de

ARVEN
School for Medicinal Plants, Aromatherapy, and Wilderness Wisdom
Postfach 24, 87475 D-Sulzberg

INDEX OF RECIPES